DICHTEN =
No. 10

No. 1: Friederike Mayröcker, *Heiligenanstalt*, 1994
No. 2: Elke Erb, *Mountains in Berlin*, 1995
No. 3: Ilma Rakusa, *Steppe*, 1997
No. 4: Ernst Jandl, *reft and light*, 2000
No. 5: Oskar Pastior, *Many Glove Compartments*, 2001
No. 6: Ludwig Harig, *The Trip to Bordeaux*, 2003
No. 7: Gerhard Rühm, *i my feet*, 2004
No. 8: Gerhard Roth, *The Will to Sickness*, 2006
No. 9: Ulf Stolterfoht, *Lingos I-IX*, 2007

DICHTEN =
No. 10

16 NEW (TO AMERICAN READERS) POETS

Burning Deck/Anyart, Providence

DICHTEN = is a (not quite) annual of current German language writing in English translation. Most issues are given to the work of a single author.
Editor: Rosmarie Waldrop.

Individual copies: $14
Subscription for 2 issues: $24 postpaid

Distributors:
Small Press Distribution, 1341 Seventh St., Berkeley, CA 94710
1-800/869-7553; www.spdbooks.org
Spectacular Diseases, c/o Paul Green, 83b London Rd., Peterborough, Cambs. PE2 9BS
HPress, www.hpress.no

for US and Canadian subscriptions only:
Burning Deck, 71 Elmgrove Ave., Providence RI 02906

Acknowledgments:
Ann Cotton's English rewrites, "Extension, Possession" and "Extroversion in Tomi," first appeared in the anthology, *Der Ficker: Second Series*, ed. Benedikt Ledebur (Schlebrügge Editor, Vienna, 2006).

Nicholas Grindell's translations of Monika Rinck, "pond too" "what it's all about," and "my thinking" were first published in *no man's land* (www.no-mans-land.org).

Tony Frazer's translation of Hans Thill's "Change of Location: the Sons" appeared in *fascicle* (www.fascicle.com); his "marsyas, encircled" by Anja Utler was first published in the Australian anthology, *Mouth to Mouth: Contemporary German Poetry in Translation*, ed. Thomas Wohlfahrt and Tobias Lehmkuhl (Giramondo, 2004).

Christian Hawkey's and Uljana Wolf's "erasures" appeared first in *manuskripte* 175 (2007).

Burning Deck is the literature program of Anyart: Contemporary Arts Center, a tax-exempt (501c3), non-profit corporation.

Cover by Keith Waldrop

© 2008 by the translators
ISSN 1077-4203
ISBN 978-1-886224-92-6

Contents

Michael Donhauser / Rosmarie Waldrop	7
Monika Rinck / R. Waldrop, Nicholas Grindell	14
Hans Thill / Tony Frazer, R. Waldrop	23
Ute Eisinger / R. Waldrop, Ute Eisinger	31
Farhad Showghi / R. Waldrop	47
Ann Cotten / Ann Cotten	50
Ron Winkler / R. Waldrop	69
Anja Utler / Tony Frazer, R. Waldrop	77
Steffen Popp / Christian Hawkey	86
Bert Papenfuss / Andrew Duncan	88
Uljana Wolf / Christian Hawkey	99
Christian Hawkey & Uljana Wolf	103
Hendrik Jackson / R. Waldrop	107
Franz Josef Czernin / R. Waldrop	111
Margret Kreidl / R, Waldrop	119
Daniel Falb / R. Waldrop	124
Raphael Urweider / R.Waldrop	133
Notes	139

Michael Donhauser

Praise Poem

So and praise to the plum trees which
And as if regained so delicate, so overhanging,
So distributed in rows, I and have searched for, so
Lost in these the streets, the language jails that
As if back and turned and an under their branches I
Now and am released, the question where and to live or
There was still a day, for in praise said he was and
Praised also the day, in the evening, the evening, the grass in tufts
The tufts and the slope strewn with clover, the clover, the
And the dandelions, the nettles in the shade, the shade
Although and the rain barrel, the loss, the table, the bench
The tables, benches and standing scattered, and the wine
The glass of wine, the word wine, the paths between, the
Between, the when, as when and the evening cool, the chirping also
The glitter also and in the sky, the sky, the twigs as
If they touched the sky, the touch, the praise, with the leaves
The leaves, the utmost, the tips of the leaves, peony leaves
And the scent of the elder, the elder, the elderwood, the soft
The wild, the umbels so full, so manifold and at the edge, the edge
To shatter, the shattering, at the instead, the instead
That would be in ivy, the ivy, the wouldbe and then the incandescent light
That the sky into the dark, the dark and comes down
Onto the trunks, the plum tree trunks that carry, the meadow, the dew
And with the dew the falling as, arrival that, the garden when
Or also the wild chervil, the also, also once more praise to and
The night, the steps, the sone, the hedgerows

The Blackbird

He, who, his, song and turned around, sings without expectation
Unless or perhaps of morning, as if song wept
In his song its eyes out and the heart of night, or as if
There were still and its infinity that he widens, warbles wide
Above the square and the roofs, across them to and over to you
As if you could and be touched by his song, or as so touched
Song you or you, where you, which you, when you as and he projects
With and in a brief twitter, between, citations that
If he breaks off it still is and then silent as if it stood and still
His song and asked where you and are, were not now or I and
A rest when you by you and as announced so turned around and here

Asline

You, language, I speak still and again
Though in words and as sung as written
So when they and rest, the crows, in a crowd or flutter
Scattered and between the lines of the vineyard or fly up
And flight after flight then and cruise in the evening
The sky, in flocks over the roofs without a wingbeat
In the wind, with the wind and caw, scream or caught
Pile up, cross over and one another with one stroke
One hesitation, so that they and as if hover, so buoyed or
Separate again and veering off veer and
Follow and singly then through the empty sky
Left behind, at a distance, so from a shadow
In motion so over the more distant, the hills, where they and
Still circle, settle, in the crowns of the trees
Of the park whence they or back they head and
Against the wind from the north until and with one last
One word like evening language still and stands still

The German title "Alszeile" also suggests a street (Zeile) in the 9th district of Vienna, called "Alsergrund" after the brook "Als."

End of Summer

After this the summer when it and comes to a halt
Still and for day after no day passes when they
The trees as if bow, so and bend on the slope and
As if driven off I and wait as if fled to the edge
So of the city, so at the edge of this summer where it is lighter
And milder so and ripened, reddened, so in the evening
The sky, when it and as begins so and blows and that
And the leaves too lift up and swing, so in the treetop
So along shoots, longer, more swaying, so and up to
Or as and if therein breathed a beginning then, there now breathes
A pull as if falling, barely already and in the plums that
And as hang so full and over and heavy, quenched with light
And swaying they too, when and again or in a cooler
A breeze the summer and declines, as inclined as and
Under the weight so of its fruit, the pears, dew-moist
With dew then, still barely moving, remembered already, so as
As a summer without stillness, without days, till and a softer
A shimmer in the pear tree, in the delicate the leaves
And shining as shines, so smiles and so also in the grass
So on the slope and transient, as if or there were still
And a reconciliation, unreconcilable, now in loss

You still and

You still and I search for
Still and in the streets that and are so overcast
In and the autumnal light, the late light when
And early so duskily as glows the sky and
Barely brighter and not brighter then than the fluorescent lights
Than the traffic lights, streetlights, headlights that
And as roam as ramble and reflect on the pavement
So and that I find again the promise, as promising
As once again and walk and along the shop windows and
Along the cars, parked or parking, that
And also seem as if and in them too were an again so
As and again in the sky that rises and toward the night
So and hovers, still, so reddish, so near death and
Near fading away, near the touch, the sound of steps that
And are echoing still, so quietly still as barely and not leading, so here
So near the edge of town, the nomore, the reconciliation, the open
So across the wide the street, so in the still before night, so when
The displays and are lying still in the light, the brighter light of the windows, so
Spotlit, so puffed up, so exhibited as if deathless and
Marked down, so instead, so that I and see them as if blessed by
So every glance and every notsaying and every justlooking and
Tirelessly so and as and if they lived in peace as things
Things within themselves and as poppy-seed cake so, as cotton jackets
As leather bags, imitation leather bags and even on the sidewalk
And ever so marked down, still or when and I and walk on and
Past also the one, the hotel where I and had lived also
So undecided also and as at that time so now I, so like the
I who so and searched for you so will so have and had

And the voices

And the voices again
Prayer voices as coffeehouse voices as
Room voices again, late afternoon voices
And the late light again the gleaming
Outside above the streets again, the
Trees, treetops and promising again
As again and as the promise of night
Of cold, deep blue, near purple, so
Near the lampshades again, the lamps that
And shine, so blinding again and pale
So remembered, so still, so as if there were also and
Consolations again, sanctifications
And proofs of love, so proven again
With the voices of fear, so hidden and
Also the handbags again, the woolen scarves
The hats, the ribbons, the indoor plants
Before winter, now, already, still
Still, now and nightly how near
The night, so again and early

And the Cherry Trees

And the cherrytrees I'll
And carry into words as they
And stand along a road or so were
Scattered over a slope a grove
And search as if and their leaves
Still rustyellow searched and the red, the red
Of their fruit, their quiet hanging, so when
And a wind shakes them or visits
The one single tree in the field that it
And as rustles so softly, so and its leaves
And come off and rise, fall and down into the grass
So leafraining, wordtired, so as and I am
And full of words I and tired and
Hardworking too, resigned too and restless
As spendthrift as seeing and that

And the Leaves

And the leaves and with the leaves a dying down
Goldyellow and mortal, yellowed a gone with the wind
In veils, whirls and upward or across the pavement
And a scent, warm, late, a loosening, a letting go
In the branches and down through the branches, that and wide
The sky and is, it seems, so turbulent now or
Deserted then when and only here and there a single leaf still
As so sinks and falls, so in falling founders: How much
You've been and a name to me and I've so also hardly
Concealed you after and all and named

Tra le due ville

That silence is
That in silence language is
As notspeaking, as stillsaying
As praise of silence
That in praise the tables are
The table cloths, table legs, table wine
The cheese cut in pieces and also the bread
The bread basket as a stillness, so and that and
Also the bats are that double back
In the sky, and the young green
Is when it shimmers on the trees
At their ends and is praised or knows
That it is and a blooming, is in clouds
In clearings of blossoms and so light
So far and near and in lamplight
And that the canopy is, the frontyard is
So and the openness, praise to being
To the chimneys in the valley, the halls, houses
The guests that arrive, the evening, the song
The open, the blackbird that and sings
So and is in the smallest cage
Where and also language, it is, so now
So and praise to it that praises being in its very perishing
Broken so, drunk in as, sung when
And with red that it and is red
The mirroring as glossy varnish, and pale
The pale as reflection of a wall or brickred
Pink and praised in geraniums

translated by Rosmarie Waldrop

Monika Rinck

pentecost peonies

in all phases of unfolding the clusters nest,
bunched packets, dense, narrow, silent
squats within buds the urge toward fat
muddled centers in purple and/or white.
back to back they sit, blossoms curving
on herbaceous stems and blooming into balls.
when it started to rain, and next to its stalk
my big hand cradled its heavy head
childhood flooded the humid air with
shrill cries of iwantiwant become a bent
with pentecostly curls. species of desire surfaced
and submerged. hearing the whispers
of the many thousand blossoms i wanted
to muss up, crumple, crush the rain-soaked
peony, pluck petals, toss them, stomp,
then call my friends, come have a look
this big fat blossomthing i have
big as a cat's head white and without eyes, me,
i want to sick the mad pack of my urges
on this cat's head that's no cat
smashed and mauled. but no, intact i leave
the solemn flowers, stiff, motionless along
the tracks my childhood races.

steals away

summer steals away with unimaginable slowness
as is the way of an inert mass
it lets rain have barcelona, lets rain have trinidad
and steals away, unimaginably slow
as is the way of an inert mass.
the sky still the same
its pallor programmatic — the heat
still the same, but heavier
and as slowly as summer there steals into
my mind what could be a foreboding,
of something bad. it could be.

that something terrible will happen, for instance
    that something timorous will happen, a parable
a blow against an inert mass
    something you cannot even feel
that leaves bodies lying in the street, leaves others behind
    and leaves drop onto the street and days lack finish
what's been turns bequest
    what's past turns perfect
as is the way of a heavy mass.
    as is the way of the past
life's still the same
    routines turn cooler
but survival programmatic — things
    and threshholds are marked — margins
still the same, but relations dissolve
    and phases flatten, turn straight as a die
and faster than foreboding stirs
    and as timorously as a parable renunciation
the last secret possibility, what's still to come
    steals into our wishing that it pass
will startle only by its mediocrity.
    it could be. it is.

park

white street lights
bundle the city and in the park
above the paths where summer's burned
rise sails of smoke.
first, my love, we'll sacrifice your chastity
and get in turn the gift of tongues
spent and relaxed our bodies lie
in the shade of speech

prolongations

that's how we stood there, we, our group
when finally the clouds arrived: heads thrown back,
arms spread like branches, hearts still
open wide with talk in warm
meadows, nights, mountains.

in the big vacation spots, la grande motte near montpellier
millions of shutters must be shut now, honeycombs
sealed from inside against a frost that doesn't exist in the south.

heavens, these straight backs, this waiting,
we, as a group, have made it so long,
long as the summer — and did we
have anxieties? not anxieties, pasts we
had, great ones and memories, each his or her own
that corner the today, what's called the now
while in the other corner squats winter at the ready.

from now on everything has consequences. belongs
to us more definitely. have we, our group
really kept it up long, really settled every-
thing? is really nothing left?

longing, they call it elsewhere and already know
it is a form of prolongation.

not having: a goal, or:
the immensely irritating bell of the lead bull

nature with hands full of dirt
barns, hayracks, the rhythm
of these awkward cottages on the slope
the edgewise fold on the neck of young bulls
entranced distances, the paths
where time unrolls,
macadamed and repeatedly remarked,
we take the slopes head on
walk in red circles with black line,
and homeward in the rope lift someone
talks of articulated structures and means
traces of snow on the rock face,
the brightness here and the dark.

not having: nature

is it the trees or is it the rain —
the unending circle of misdemeanors
and counting them. *patience*. a large —
an imagined herd, an open form made of
so many animals and their movement toward
something, the culling maws, and almost
within reach, between the bodies
there shows, suddenly, in the venal light
of wandering beasts, all that is lacking.
ah, *le paysage* and the experience
of saying yes, a spacious country house
rented to help my thinking so poor in objects —
and it would learn, yes, i promise
it would, as if with hands of its own
to open the pod, the very green, as if by itself,
synchronous in all respects and like antennae tactile,
spreading in the air the animals breathe.

not having: substances (this is for paddy)

out went the mixer of poisons in early evening
i trailed her or she tailed me.
impossible to decide in the quantum
mechanics of the present. what's wrong
knows discrete packets, ponchos, things at once
in two places or more, stairwells,
and the city, the city when it rains,
comforting, cooling. i want to trail her and the world,
want where wish and addiction inherit each other
where body sloughs off thought like bark, and the naked
barrel trunk would stand in the shadow of its wind-walloped crown
and withdrawal so chemical, so flat, so wonderfully there.

green faces: are we just something in space

we imitated interstellar nebulae,
a cosmic rabble, the camera was on,
but something seemed to be in the air,
or maybe rather on the lens,
this deep lack of focus as if
our very perceptions were affected and
we could no longer count on them.
scattered energy, wait
between scenes, long treks
down the obsolete hall. the sandwiches
we ate, rugs in beige and brown,
dirt, whole layers, I thought, of
who knows what, here had perhaps
precipitated of all possible feelings only
the wrong ones and formed sediments. "cut!"
we looked at one another. faces reflecting
greenish light, underneath like growing silence
the carpet. ugh, what filthy hues.

schwedenschanze gentlemen I

we talk of the set of analyzable things with horns
that browse on moss and sparse herbs in ownerless lots.
next to the set of legends of which we do not talk
because we can't. but look, brother, the mountains!
the dry tops of the firs, the snowwhite peaks,
the rumbling of impending falls, the mangy bears,
the muttering of the rescue squad, the term for airplane
fuel that won't cross the good herdsman's lips.
my brother whittles while i talk, up high
my voice but a hair in the dark fir ridge.
of the huge goat herd i talk, that crossed over into the
condition of sheep: the steep line of each goat's eyelid,
of its pupil, flipped blindly into the horizontal.
from this lateral beam there sprouted the flat sheep-look.
clacklack. a very secret mechanism, a sound as from the knees
of many thousand pilgrims accompanied the transition.
valleys curved into pastures, luscious, deep gorges no longer
offered shelter. my brother won't accept this:
"my dear," he says, "there are clouds that bring good
weather and clouds that bring bad. the set of those for which
it is true that they bring both, must needs be empty.
this holds as much for sheep and goats even should they
graze on the threshold to the other species." but i
did hear the sound from their eyes and will never
forget it. the trim goats on the peaks, in the thin air
of god's nearness, were rounded into sheep feeding below
the knee-timber zone, covered with wool instead of fur.
my new sheep move in herds along the line of difference
and say baa. it's certain they wear mourning
or perhaps some rare equivalent.

translated by Rosmarie Waldrop

cooperation

he cooperated with ships, with temperatures,
with sirens and with the neighbourhood, he multiplied
the hours of my wakefulness by abandonment.
the tense, restless sleep that discharged me,
always too early, into vertical hours, half-light
i stood in the twittering like steel or seaweed.
and my lover was ocean. i did not rust.
instead, it was the salty water that rusted.
guess that's the way. in the hyperrealism cabin.
but i glided. did early things in the early hours.
i kept a lookout, too, and i took a look at him,
as if standing on slopes, on waves,
on light or on forces. on gales. only then
did land appear and there was a tolling of bells,
though dawn had been so long ago.

pond too

in the place where once was something
the hollow fills to form a pond.
the water is immediately blackish.
stagnant. in it, imagined, firs.
blackish too. and closely packed.
what comes next happens once a dozen years:
at the centre, the void rises up
meniscus-like and hoists the spot
furthest from the banks into a hook.
thus, finally, the sunken shore
reappears, consisting of:
rot-black moss,
distempered fauna
and something like caoutchouc.

what it's all about

a whole landscape of ponds,
pale grey loam, mountains of building rubble,
then the insects, very large dragonflies,
hovering flat out, buzzing.
crossed skeeters use the matte varnish
of the collected water to leap from,
to land on. a ruffling. a trilling.
then their predators, the frogs
and, at the end of the chain, us too.
we walk. wade. drag our feet so.
who'd have thought it so hard to walk, so slow,
with tired, tired out knees.
the leaps. the landing. the foul sheen
on the water. the slightest touch,
such a sudden shove, minuscule rings.
atoms vibrate, vibrate in the neutral position.
frogs swallow. dragonflies. then us again.

my thinking

today, around lunchtime, i saw my thinking,
it was a meadow, grazed bare, with hummocks. though
it could have been foothills of moss-covered mountains,
the kind of fuzzy green carpet fed on by reindeer.
no, just a busily bulging landscape beyond
the tree line, and it sure was close-cropped.
the thoughts passed over it, a little light-headed,
like currents of air made visible, no, more
like a fleet of immaterial hovercrafts. they used
the hummocks   as ramps.

the fount of teachings

to no avail i ask the driver for a light. to no avail
i stack things my way, my ankles, white and red.
that's the cartilage, the leverage. turn left after the prison.
where shal l i store this humiliation away?
do i save it under person or function —
a question, conflicting and neutral in every respect.
that's just the dilemma. raise the playing field,
alter the standards, or find something
that helps escape them. or just look on, unmoved,
immunized by rage? i mean, should i purge myself?
you know what, my actual job is church father,
this passenger thing is just a disguise. and so i say unto you:
as well as the five senses that point outwards
you have, according to origen, five more senses
that point inwards — a bit further down
wilsnacker strasse — and only when you lose these,
too, can you start over again from the beginning.
there will be other people to love you, presumably.
but take a look at me, what you see here
in the rear-view mirror is my second last face
for producing sensorially perceptible fullness of time,
that's all there is. keep the change, goodnight.

translated by Nicholas Grindell

Hans Thill

Change of Location: the Sons

1
WHILE walking one shook
his scrawny frame and on horseback
he was a naked nine
his brother let fields wither
that he planted a third lay
between two mountains harking
to the rockface

In the wet everyone ducked
humbly into the tent smoked the
peace-pipe with bent backs

2
FROM FAR OFF came a relative
and the sons made music, first
honking horns through the streets then the listeners
stacked the trashed hall furnishings
right behind the stage. On this evening each man
wore his shortest shirt

3
THE SONS spent their childhood hanging
head-first from horses their blonde manes
growing up against the steppe-grass
intertwined in sleepless nights with the
flax of girls who listened out
for neighbourhood bawling

4
AT MIDDAY the sons lay next to one another
like signs in the sand. They formed a quick prayer
from right to left, repeated from left to right.
From the ocen side a wet push drove
into their bodies and made them illegible

5
THE SONS' ENEMIES came off ships
approached the village palisades by night
with childlike cries seized the strongest animals
and disappeared into the desert

6
THE SONS and their painted women
who sat in provocative poses on the freshly-laid table
while their spouses bent over topographical
sketches. Field telephone / rushing the
guests / departure. The red pennant
high up above the animals

7
ON WEARY FEET and up to the ankles
in sand the sons brought their children
salty bleeding food. Comrades rescued
from distress were dried out for three days
in the marketplace. Before they
broke camp to folllow the cars
into the marshes the sons allowed
their dogs to roam all night long
through the dwellings

8
IN THE MARSHES there was food
and water to excess. The sons fled
from the mosquitoes up to the karstic
plateau until they could no longer bear
the herd's hunger cries

9
TO THE SINGING of their red-haired women
the sons sponged their animals clean.
The washing ended with the women
falling silent. Resin that dropped
from the trees was used
and the ashes from past times.
Also they patched up the tent or other sky roofs
singing their siren song

10
ON THE WAY to the waterhole
the sons died.
No one could accuse them of
last words. Those standing around
said their farewells with a handshake.
Now and then a fighter jet howled
over the tents

                              translated by Tony Frazer

from *If Only I Were Fever*

BEING A GUEST: Sneakers that pushed us into the pillows. His you're-welcome as literal as his striped socks gathering dust on the tracks. And his stamp-pad smile: a minister's kiss! But in conversation he proved a tough priest who sat tight on his cashbox. A funeral barker who's urned his bitters. Hard to hold down with hoopla or frown. When sneakers threatened we summoned veins of anger. Somebody showed his biceps: a bluff counted in degrees latitude hence ball-shaped. Sneakers reared demanding sugar and snapped up nuts. We hadn't yet scooped everything onto torture when he swerved for camomile tea, which we parried in our best Greek: coughs we knew like the back of our hand! Now lightning! he whispered, collared, when we pulled the strings and him straight to his company car

DINGY WINDOWS thinned with bars befingered with screens like couples in a copse? Fucking behind facades does not require illumination. The plants are hollow it makes you want to howl. If someone here squeezes out a tear it's the thinner that chases couples into the trees. Another silently picks windfalls in the gloom. A red velvet beadle a crammer for clergy an old lech who lists and greases his wheezes on every hill? Malicious before the fall. Eden? oblivious whisper and whizzing under leaves in a cone of wind or light if someone happens to snap his fingers. O-la-lalling Paris where so many thirsty couples and strictly speaking but 1 prick to pin 1 flesh to thin however much it may weigh. The lighting is poor. The waitress now rattly now fat. The windows stilted

LEGIBLE on his sorrow's knees he was cold comfort. With his left he dried the tears his right had squeezed out while everyone was watching. What had chased him from his lair: trenchant tropics? Melancholy among rubble all too clearly undecided when to praise: for a bow and scrape we had summoned him, now not even a hosannah's left. At best the ablaze from his right knee the red cock conflagration crowing Roger! At best a leg of the footstool on which he wept for his widow: if only I were fever

ITEM in each quarry we had put aside an ashlar. We stacked with ease. Something slid off the table certain to fall on our bones. Every step was a confession every sentence began with Adam. Many jumped on A others controlled themselves. Even before the revolution we stand before the Palatine sound-apple but the lines are laid the system known. Item we called Adam Adam

ADAM'S APPLE was sick of dyspepsia a gurgling movement through the esophagus into which we kept shouting gums! or a rattling movement over to N.Y. Sliver stuck in the throat Eve had a drop too many and read IRREAL for ISRAEL. He motionless, string wandering instead of apple stops occasionally in places of bangbang. Stop Hadam! cried –white comically, but he already stood, no, lay in the glass coffin. The media complained that 'snow' was missing. Now Cain whom Adam had clearly forgotten to core was supposed to stretch but wanted praise wanted to be breathed

BREATH one wants to cry while having sex or baking pretzels like greased lightning but chances are against it. No merry frost this unrepentant flatus no London captain versed in fact. During smog put on your smoking jacket or you'll swallow the inch of indignation. Sic! one wants to say but not with dentures. Mine and mine we run through the samples as the masthead invites us to. After all we're sweaty from work. The mills do badly a chance for pretzels would be an opinion in your sleep for which we'd have to breathe. We don't do away with ourselves. More matter and above all louder! we were supposed to whisper and clap our hands assuming we were among the invited. Hoarse singer an air mattress in his merriment. Spitter kicker genuine greased pretzel sex! we might grumble but it all comes down to meta-breath that we'd like to exclaim

---

The Palatine sound-apple: North of Karlsruhe runs the so-called "Appel-Apfel line." South of it the fruit is pronounced "Apfel," North of it, "Appel."

IT TAKES two to spit: one to curl the tongue and a racketeer best from the Far East: wasn't it there this sudden snowman who spent the voyage bent over the railing was later puffed into an ocean giant? One catches the mouth projectile the other hops the most squares possible till scotched. Yeti from Peking still pale among the audience tipped willy-nilly onto dry land: a cellulose goobye and a nivea welcome. Let's not skimp on water now! the Americans applaud in groups of three almost an insult almost already a sandwich

VANILLA alias convent dust or today let's knot a windsor tie. We make the sign of the cross and take the first turn back out. On pentecost we go glue tongues. We rob the fire of its sweetness, but our speech is licked into shape. The apostles babble praise the boss while the sergeant orders retreat or procession. The Romancaths keep ringing bells. Bend their knees at every vanilla. We grip the loop with thumb and index: head over backwards and through below. A waffle for every smile! begs the colonel of the backbone that he waves about. We backpedal and squeeze our neck till it fits. How many revolutions per minute does a Tartuffe carry in his shirt? Depending on the density the aroma hums on the lower lip roars like Don Camillo at the dentist clings to the palate and goes down with bells on. We pull at the lower loop until it wriggles. Blessed by whipping cream. Who will take this stain to his breast? A confessor or condom. A cloud of black points thrives in barracks hence flowers a monstrance and for all I care. Down with it for a while

from *Malignant Eden*

ALLEGEDLY took on the Stroke and counted his drops. Never had he been so shy of company. Was dragged along the roads later shown also on wheels (our picture). But no pity for Allegedly. More and more often tried to shake without regard to the label. True, along with his host Stroke destroyed his own home. Allegedly was swindled on the high sea while the guest still managed quickly to achieve a smoker's leg. Was levered soundlessly mouth nose pushed under the salty surface. Minerals no use for Stroke Allegedly hated rings around his hips. An end in lederhosen was in sight: Stroke saved Alledgedly ruined. Or the opposite corpus callosum solution. A tale's a tale. Freestyle or hypochondria? Hiccup or chuckup?

NOTSOBAD a generation better off sleeping. Yet behind frosted glass fared like shy fish. If and But slept more lightly though less ostentatiously. Gathered and yawned their Notsobad. A mutt from every village? Late in the year were awakened with a feminine Don't Bend. A spouse calling often and gladly a sine qua non for the whole generation.

PETTYTHEFT compared a vulture's cry to the bleat of a curly lamb. Not in my basket! said the juror with oathy face. Master Higgins missed peeps and strayed into aviaries. Pettytheft took what flew out

Higgins was stuck with shoplifting. Arrested he proved a fallacy. The fox! fluted the geese. Pettytheft was bothered by the white coats. After hours many walk with red hair. Higgins and Pettytheft? precious precious

BITTERLY and the thrice denied nine. He gave in and paid. Yet more competently crowed the cock. Bitterly denied again but this time with a check. Plucked clean reacted with insomnia. In front of open windows a bechickenwinged Easterly flew through the valley with a splinter relieved itself

Easterly's influence: last a gardener's soul buried deep down with the talents. His forebearance fell among Bitterly's wrinkles and vice versa. Whoever rested by the wayside wore sandals with Samaritan bands. Thus Easterly strapping and dusty like grammar Bitterly still shaking his head. In preparation: other numbers other conditions

DIETRICH was lit up in cloudy weather. You'd see the street lead in broad daylight to a cloudy Dietrich. Your hand before your eyes you reached as far as her utmost high heel. There light burst from all the tubes: legs up to the ears? Arms spread wide? Atlantic crossing? You saw the angel saw the spot saw the trickle. Shivering you honked your horn. Turned off. A black cat was mixed into the dark. You got a dent from this beast of the deep. Then knocked on the wreath and went in

WOODEN a silly fiddle half hermitage half living room fir. Up from the underworld it had oozed truant and tragic. The men hummed and sank into the shade of their cool. Not to be confused with leisure time according to Gertrude Stein! Why else would the whole continent have tried to rattle her? In the middle she was sugar and in the center she drank pop. Frequently moved she was called liquid bride. Porte parole! as our speaker nasalized. A tip for death at dawn! said the stock exchanger. Idiomatically this was a sketch and joke. Sparkling the tears she swallowed, wintersplit the ground on which she slid. Alas her tailored body was no flimsy rag as she stood at the harbor. But the sky was full of hats and all around her frigates tooted: tanga tanga! and whatever else was on the roster

translated by Rosmarie Waldrop

Ute Eisinger

Cusp

¡Ay!

Each Other's Wonder

TrajectoryARC							Transparency

Each Other's Wound

Ultramarine

Direction, Place

Cusp

¡Ay!

Each Other's Wonder

Transparency

Each Other's Wound

Ultramarine

Direction, Place

My brother's run meets,
   where the ball hits, in pre-kick league,
     pre-sonic, a tone.
        "As turns in flight?" — stops.
     Vault betrays echo.
    Struts drive deep
into the ground.

Cusp

¡Ay!

Each Other's Wonder

Transparency

Each Other's Wound

Ultramarine

Direction, Place

For a call to project its parabola
   out of the blue night olive grove,
      a rainbow,
         it takes two mountains (two mountains);
      so that, as loose wind strings quiver
   under the violin bow,
cave dwellers raise their flares.

Cusp

¡Ay!

Each Other's Wonder

Transparency

Each Other's Wound

Ultramarine

Direction, Place

"That you read me
   as I read you
      is
         a wonderful arc
      that in a wondrous way
   more and more closes with each day,
with each end of a beautiful day."

Cusp

¡Ay!

Each Other's Wonder

Transparency

Each Other's Wound

Ultramarine

Direction, Place

The air jangles with swallows;
    Like open books
        they swim the sky blue,
            hairline crannies, ink jam
            chain in their wake
            winged twin oars
        burst open the stream.

Cusp

¡Ay!

Each Other's Wonder

Transparency

Each Other's Wound

Ultramarine

Direction, Place

(That I should read you
　　as you would reach me
　　　would
　　　　　be the end of an arc that
　　　　in an endemic way
　　　more and more abrades with each day,
with each end of a fearful day.)

Cusp

¡Ay!

Each Other's Wonder

Transparency

Each Other's Wound

Ultramarine

Direction, Place

Two mountains for the blue arc!
    Out of the clear night rises, falls
        — olive gooseflesh to witness —
           the call. Wind-strung a violin bow took it up
      and ripples on the lake,
   and from around the incidence
simply clears out.

Cusp

¡Ay!

Each Other's Wonder

Transparency

Each Other's Wound

Ultramarine

Direction, Place

I know the reach of the arrow
   my brother shoots;
      at the place it hit I found my cue.
         Everything had its direction.
         With a fitting word I'll find the place
      that closes with my sister,
I know the safe load of the pier row.

translated by Rosmarie Waldrop

from LEG O BLOCKS

The Art of Sailing

To anticipate static means reading the tuning knob.
  The overturns of the high flow crest
    to elude, easily slicing, rise.
      Harnessing currents — the art of sailing.

Clear, settle

The tunes of outpour shimmer with dryness, held
  Into light: their final relief by the law of time.
    As underflowing and overbrimming
      Lament or ferment settle in wines.

Fishbones chiming. Numb lupines defying frost.
  A blinding deceit of stars exchanged
    For needle, stone, strings. The towering
      Lighthouse tensing cold sinews.

Discerning the times makes the ears ring.
  The impact of stars to be bound
    Elegantly, close their sling, to
      futural present: sore and evil.

translated by Ute Eisinger

Farhad Showghi

End of the City Map

1

THE CITY MAP comes to an end. Extrovert steppe- and pillow-fires, marches across soil for onions and cedars. We try something, know names, but what arrives is landscape. If you answer in time you cross into the neighbor's garden and become a snowball bush. In uncertain if self-reliant manner. No window steps out of line with its silence and our words. Nobody takes houses or front yards on a fishing trip. Noonday water trickles through sunlit tops of plantains. More easily than a hand from a pocket escapes the vast distance. The hand opens. Poise of a service road. That soon reverts to thinking.

2

I NO LONGER KNOW, because the city is still there, where my mouth opens most naturally, worth seeing: the fiber wallpaper, but window and sun shine asunder, nobody makes the effort to stand still, no skin in shoes, very patient with our limbs we hold on to the doors when the houses flow across the front yards as is their habit, in flux to stay ahead of us.

3

A RUCKUS OF ROOFS is what the South is about, bright red smoke from the earth that retreats where we suspect a zone of window congestion, looking up through groups of notched pines, cabbage and cockle come to light, sheep-clatter, shouts, and we recite the city by heart, farther down the street, would that be an announcement? a pronounced, resolute wind, as we leave the house, makes us more visible than the doorbells.

4
WHEN THE MOON promises good lighting for hands, a cross path on the quiet eating white-footed nests. We hear the city, fold the laundy.

5
WHAT NOW? The city learns from the sky, calms itself down. Sheltered gardens surrender their entire silent distance. When we cannot hold on to this movement we weigh ourselves down with our voices. Let's try. To get a silence for ourselves that moves on our feet. Where we do not say anything a calm hand claims the harbor. Seven, eight gulls keep a sightseeing flight awake. As the East on the right and on the left the South. Even a false estimate can end up with ships. When cranes turn shy the clouds drift off.

6
FINGER ON A GRAIN of asphalt, my voice approached. I entertained the distance, backyard turbulence gathered warm, strongly lit streets. Trees came back to me. To reach up to the birds I had to make a giant mistake.

7
WITH GAS and water separate houses take new positions. In front of a distance. That misses itself and hoards lifeless skies. We draw a language, read a name, ring the bell and wait. The moon still clings to the body, its garden system shining among the poor. We hear children moving rooms, simplified rules of the game behind a lightly timbered door. Evening light has grown voices with feet.

8
NO DOUBT: Calming down with whole names the streets returned from the water. Prone to flightiness, houses could start anywhere. A gateway in back often used daylight. I could not with shadows and shoes mend the madness of roused foliage. For precipitous backyards the harbor air exerted itself to the innermost. Burped a jittery heaviness. I am used to the window. To one sky or another, and sing the window as well as myself. Should the window suddenly slow down I'd be stuck, waiting room among chestnut branches.

9

LET'S LOOK BEHIND many houses for the point where the city's name begins. Whence we again know a few streets we can drive up or down, slowly in the cool air, while others already turn off, spots of light and parking gravel let us go, then we also like to live around, and perhaps from afar a hand comes, waves, has cooked for us in north or south.

10

I OPEN SOMETHING, but sunlight loosens my shoulderblade. A grocery store lit up, vulnerable, rocking in the neighbor's yard. Now I walk along the street in conversation with shrubs and salads, and the line bus turns into a quick garden. Nice day, you have to count on airplanes breaking small white fingers, we say, this way the blue starts, worth getting hurt for, the air is good and audibly affects my sweater chest. A residential block with its windows and doors goes right through me, ringing, down to my ticket hand. And right away I start having my accident.

trans. Rosmarie Waldrop

Ann Cotten

Homology, Myself

If I were a robot, I would rule
myself, my limbs, the USA.
Would wipe all differing schools
and borders off the walls. I'd be

here solo, soiled and oiled. Conditions
would leave me cold and indeterminate.
It's cool. It's nominal. So much
depends on arguments that

turn out void when looked at closely;
when listened to, too stale; tasted, too dense;
dropped in the slot come out dispensed.
I cannot smell what looks at me, nothing
I hear tastes good. Things don't come near
what I want, till my nose says: anything goes.

I would be supple, if I were like myself.
This way I grimly scrutinize my poses
which likewise grimly hint that I have lost it.
Though blindly thus I pick up my own tricks

I'd still be wrong and none the wiser for my pains
would follow sleepily the brain-lint's blueprint.
No thanks to hints: the stripes remind me of
the angelfish that circles in its tank. For every

thousand times it bangs it head against the glass
automatons could bang a million.
I'm not like robots, am not even like myself,
and when I contradict my tongue, my tongue
cried treason, though it's with me like a nosy parrot
and on good days will let me taste its freedom.

Ingeniously Recognize

May I compare the summer's day to you?
It ends while I my sonnet first try.
Beginning a sonnet while the day goes by
may I compare the summer's day to you?

My fear the page might yellow and decay
on which your gold curdles to blue
fades as your profile's contour turns more true
and words resemble, similes agree with you.

First of all, it is now May,
your radiance without shade is
just like a sun no one has tired of.

Second, your hair's like flax, your mouth
like clouds through which the sun bursts
flaunting brute force as in summer.

And like high noon your body blazes
square and planned with ingenuity,
your eye cut out as if from blasphemy.

True and present, as long as I am here
I implement desire, puncture silence.
You don't lack place, nor I, the way
to soothe your surface onto paper.

And should you perish or just go away
thanks to this crib I know all that is true.
New generations will approximately see you
and I shall always recognize a summer's day.

Yearning, Webcam

A lightweight plastic eye surveys your chamber.
Flesh is too grand to look at faulty skin.
The mechanisms make my optic nerve grow thinner,
grey matter turn to carbon. All I want

is a glance that's mobile, what
anyone can see of you without
turning around. If there's a flicker
on the screen I think you have manipulated

the dead spot so I can't see you making out
— your body, which I know, is growing dimmer —
with your girl. However, when you used to lie
close by my side, wrapped in your sleep,
I didn't see you either. My eyes missed you
however urgently they snapped at you.

So you manipulate this borrowed carbon, then
avoiding the thin cables of my phantasy,
the imaginary eye that feasts and feeds on you
longingly shapes the misty images, as when

you groped one morning for your glasses
to shoot a piercing look at me. How with one jerk
of the knee you rode your chair toward the desk
to stop the repeat long gone berserk.

Your laptop softly clicked while we were mingling
secretions, rhyme, slime, sameness. Saw us
talking quietly, and on us sweat and light
and air with breath, and eyes with too fast closing
fists. And with a hum announced: all lust is blind,
but yearning sees the past and touches with precision.

He Says He Finds the Term Questionable

When gleaming your skin   moved apart from mine
and dreaming your mouth   knows words in your sleep,
and sleeping your shoulders   have sought out my sheet
to lie on tonight,   now prone now supine;

when ticking the clock   churns the hours of night,
and sleeping your ear   burns into my eye,
and dreaming your hand   finds itself on mine
making my dreams   dive close to my thought

then I may think   of this half-baked poem,
how it'll turn out,   but instead see your face,
its bone structure   salient in sleep,

and see your temple   where the dim light plays
and watch your breathing   and hold my breath
expecting some depth   from these your traits.

For the world's weight   embroils your breast.
In the half-light   your ribs are creaking.
In the skipped beat   I almost kissed – but halt:
my muse's lips   are moving.

You ask me why   my eyes are open.
I close them quick: "I am asleep."
You ask me how   page-foolish time
flows second-wise.   I tell you I,

to cultivate leisure   while heaven dozes,
to grasp your thinking,   manage the dark,
and in infrared   develop thought
exposures till   light turns to words,
till this proud mess   forgets to breathe:
And ask my muse   what the hell a muse is.

Thoughts Cubital

As if there were a corner in my thinking or
a leak along the line from mind to brain;
as if something were hotwiring my optic nerve,
the dendrites in confusion, twisted, flying

around like flies just learning how to fly,
awkwardly spreading their synapses, then
hitting the wall, stall, reel with bumps
the size of goose-eggs — and consider leaving...

Thoughts, go ahead and go, you're free,
free as mosquitoes; I no wiser than before,
slapping at thoughts smash my own ear,

and laughing shrilly mash my head to mud,
like St. Sebastian turn my eyes toward heaven,
and, bleeding to death, in rapture cry for more!

You have to earn your poses roughing it.
The way they look at you initially suggests
a hope of getting help as long as you're
ready to sell your thoughts for love

when favor turns away. And nearly everything
is open wide, shoots peas, and doesn't fit.
Being springy like the backbone of a fly swat
authorizes every one to hit me. Fuck it!

I'm not leaving here, no not never ever
(confirms, with boy sopranos, dendrite choir).
Here is the spot at which I lost my mind
because some pretty asshole recognized my kind
and took advantage of my eyes that can't conceal
that I, when faced with beauty, tend to kneel.

Standstill, Teleological

When you, toward eight, begin to lick your candles, -
like moments small in far-away gondolas –
and light their alphabet and know the shuddering aureolas
are, in whatever order, "simply beautiful,"

and I along the edge of consciousness
noticing candles tittering at my neck,
maneuver toothless loss of face, my doubts
concerning movement filter cynically

your skills, lamed by your hand's familiar formulae.
I'm only paper, what are you trying to say?
Fallen beforehand, the untaken-back reply
conveys befuddlement. It seems as if
you're talking to yourself in outer space:
"A: man. B: different. Anyone listening?" fades away.

Scattered all over the space that now surrounds us
are pillow covers and the draft small fires make.
If our goal drifts off, the sparks will soar
clear out of time. It is uncanny.

It startles me and glues my eyelids shut.
I'm hardly I when I awake out of this seam
shouting: "Houdini here! Go blast the corsets!"
They've long been burst. With you. New idioms

need be got, meta-in-motion, a springing up
of naked drives to cross synaptic corpses
and suck our way toward vacuum.
No black hole knows our games. It must
make way for our tremendous gift of gab: dumb
as it gives the slip to the oblique, our goal likes cheek.

Extension, Ecstasy

Click. It where began to turn
show up on banks and thus
the river. Anorganic, luminescent,
anger merely on the surface where

raged and unattainably shrill
turned, and light sprayed,
spattered, therefore while I must laugh,
to lick the banks began, light, gentle.

The eyes done started it.
Mouth, naw, don't get a thing. Is fulla
hairs, they fight the tongues
for recognition, demanding
the attention of the eyes. No go.
When mere extension tries to stretch to ecstasy

each sentence must stand fast, eyes peeled,
must widen the horizon into ground,
on which these wild expansion-thoughts entwine
small, perhaps white stones.
The eye chews long on this mirage,
on glints that flit across the surfaces

and say what we can never get our tongue
around repeating. Here, lungs,
hold still and watch how it goes to
the head of your, yes, clientele. How

the grey cells pant after the correspondences
that haunt your shticks and search
for kicks. Hey, lungs, wanna do something fun?
Go breathe the glistening water, lungs.

To a Waltz, Whiskey

Sleep is a doll too small for your arm,
yet in it you try to dissolve.
Daylight is pushing your eyes toward me:
you wish it, but won't get involved.

Hey, life is as bright as a courtyard at six,
a wall can keep weariness under a lid,
and it's clear as air that your heart overflows,
but how tell this to the kids?

Say goodnight, lay your head on the waltz and its beat,
give my forehead a nice wet kiss,
take your dress off my darling, let's call it a day,
though the daylight is slow going away
and the cat's killing pigeons outside, still at play
with the mice, little one, feel the teeth?

Oh I'm sick at heart as the evening lightly
sweeps into my ear with the waltz's old score.
Say just one word, close my eyes with your hands.
When Katrinka's asleep we'll sneak out the door.

Doleful as the Fates, with groaning shoes
(the waltz in the courtyard now numb as a newt)
you'll quietly on the way out grab the whiskey
and everything rises to double and wings.

When we no longer see things and foolishly stand
in the light from the windows of neighbors who read
the waltz is a spin in our heads without sound –
then think of Katrinka who dreams in her bed,
o think of Katrinka, just recently born:
her boat will ride steady although we go down.

Sirens in the Age of Mechanical Reproduction

To rage against beauty is my task as a girl,
to demolish impressions and set sweet men askew
who startle me with beauty until I make confessions.
Though I attempt a snarl, I'm gaping at the view

that snags me like a cogwheel. They tied me to the mast
but stronger is the word that binds me to the man.
Fed up with moderation, congested quandaries:
I'm stranded in mid-ocean, my mind is going fast.

Come here, sweet thing, and don't turn on the light.
Where are you? Here! You cannot see my teeth
in the dark, but feel them as they pierce
your layers. Now you believe me? No, can't get it right, I
only see grey padding. Where's your face?
Can you come closer? Damn, I need more light.

Back home I plug the printer in to print him.
The printer prints in stripes, omits now reds
and now the blues. That's how it goes whenever I
produce a version. Must have to do with copyright.

But I am in possession of a pair of cardboard glasses:
One lens is blue, the other red, for seeing 3D.
I put them on and grin insanely: Finally I see
the guy I cloned, whose features had impressed me.

Without your voice you no longer bewitch me.
Beauty's enough, though, to make me perish, not
in ice, nor yet in heat, just in a sea
of inane darkness, stubborn visuality.
As your voice in the dark sealed my enchantment with your face,
its beauty makes its case: it's you will have to ditch me.

Extension, Possession

Your name's all over the place, and yet there was a time,
I mean, not long ago you were a new lesion.
And now I hardly see a word without seeing
you in the place of everything I miss. Laughter

falls at your feet and leaves you standing stark naked
What does this mean? Five minutes ago you were a stranger
and now you wear cheap sonnets wreathed
around your name. You throw them on the ground and leave.

The only thing that's left is leaving's imagery
to fling my verses at and sing the praises of your back,
perhaps the nicest part of you or, rather,
all I can sing about now that you're gone. I track
daydreams in lines, I trace your nose, but will not say
your name out loud. In writing then? Forget it.

But still: in every foreign word I hear your voice calling
me back, which would be better, though your back is lovely.
Meanwhile every day I deal in idle prattle,
handing out trite lines to all the wrong people

and poke and puke in quiet tests of verse
that won't shine even half as bright as your silence.
And so I use the back you turned on me, smiling,
as static model for my ideal constructions.

If you, prism, distort the world I live in,
I still know your name, and love in vain
its sound, tougher than peals of laughter in
the face of my attempts. A stray, strange word
brings back your face: smiling, promising
nothing but sonnets and refusing to explain.

Content, Teleological

Why would you want to make a try at content?
As soon as you begin, you go half crazy,
amazed at the decay that starts to mould
the thought you see you might have meant.

Like: prams cruising in the square like whales,
and you slip past as if it wasn't your idea.
You have to fill your images with mind,
give them direction, not just atmosphere,

and buckle in the backlash of the terms you place.
No longer be content with a pretty face
or ass, lipservice ringing changes on quotations.
Esteeming content doesn't mean talk it into bed
or be talked into someone else's, and describe it.
What yearning dictates will be biased information.

Begin with where you are, with right beside you,
with where you turn around and see the flights
of paths, the draughts tried by your thoughts
and sobbing, counting, follow in their steps.

Concreticize genetics from whatever,
shuffle it, split it, recombine the parts,
abandon reproduction. If you must, write poems.
And don't shove them in front of you like prams.

Appreciate their eye, learn their baleen, and feel
their pulse next to your chin. Behind their pupils
look for the blackbox that conceals
all the details. Everything is more specific
than you can ever understand, but words
are cared for by themselves, just like the whales.

Sixteen, Too Angry to Bluff Snuff Cuff Rough Love Stuff's Tough Enough

kein schimmer! dumm, trüb, krumm, lieb wimmert glimmen immer schlimmer
and time should be illusion of dishonesty?
Who's whispering these words in my hormone-suspended thinking,
what demons would so twist my head and watch me sink?

The words are technoid, contained and areodynamic.
I happen to be hanging out in math, toward end of class,
engraving robots in my desk, and when they ask,
I pry pine nodules from my nails and say something semantic.

Time be illusion of what? dishonesty?
I don't believe this (in what person) sentence.
What does it crow about, here from another time,
why can't they spend their time with problems of their own?
I'll be alright. I've never yet complained.

Behind the scenes this sentence's trying to disarm me.

au schau bau zeug beug frau klau rauch mach heute blau
Haven't the foggiest idea who must be fought,
I'll punch into the mist and hope I hit.
They all deserve it, hope it helps.

I hear my footsteps run, hope I don't lose my pneum.
My footsteps thunder through the bell for break:
Please find me, stinking old pneum, please come;
yesterday you were almost here, only I got scared.

Now I'm beheading dandelions by the rotten gate
and killing time by making some pretense.
I walk fast as if this weren't my own turf, I'm late
and prick my ears to pierce the intersecting bells
and hear: Time is illusion of dishonesty.
And can't but scream and let go of my shell.

Extroversion in Tomi

toast pops up, rattling my silence

My mind goes coffee coffee coffee coffee
I'm leaving out several thoughts

that someone in the street might not relate to.
I think about   which was
something I didn't want to think about.
My life gets more absurd with every day.

Oh god, why isn't my Corinna here? I swore
last night that I can't take it, cannot breathe,
this place makes me throw up.
The people in the street consider me an accident.
The other day my shirt was buttoned wrong.
I even hate the rhymes now, kick them in the teeth.

The DVDs, the ones Corinna sent me,
been using them as saucers for my cups
and threw the others   at the fucking cat
miaowed when I jerked off holding Corinna's picture.

Now even the cat won't look at me.
Last night, or was it the one before? down at the only joint
I knocked the leader of the auxiliary fire brigade
all bloody in a fight. So I can't go there anymore.

I refrain from thinking more and more,
leave out all words beginning with a C
and all   containing double n.
Corinna, sugar, listen, my novel may revert
to nought. Because I work
on cutting   all the bits that hurt.

Sound Synthesis, Digital

Whoah, where are you, coder, coder, whoah!
I was asleep. I heard your fingers drumming
as if a membrane loose in space were thundering.
Now woken up, don't recognize you. Lost

in ether so much vital information
and all that's left is data, easily confused.
My ears take you in ever more faintly,
my programs imitate you with attrition.

O mode vocis, cymbals, tympanons demand you.
Why, coder, d'you get distorted when I understand you?
Is it too retro to so adamantly want you?
The dry and faintly clattering sound scrutinizes
sound waves that seldom ever redden at the
brink, but overwhelm and overtake me.

Echo hears Echo calling: read me, Narcissus?
Narcissus: All I'm getting's Echo. Echo: Over.
Stuck in reverb, halting in space, they mean
so well, but have bad ears. Morose

and boring more and more, they drag their circuits
round the world. They're getting on each other's nerves.
But only recently has a dissolve turned digital.
Echo and Narcissus feel they're slipping out of reach.

Subject: Re: rem conquassatam, but no meeting
as delays used to be, now unsubstantial,
each sits in his own time, insanely busy,
is ready any time for an immediate answer.
They build up sound from one another's noises,
modern, as if something were the matter with their voices.

Nonesuch I

The ghost came to me as a kind of shirt.
Someone had hung it by the dancefloor and it was
everything's opposite. Odd but true. How strange,
how downright weird it sounds when I tell how it was.

Something was wrong with what I was working on
those days. Time seemed to have something in mind,
wrung my bones and gloated over how I spent it,
squeezed my guts to get something it couldn't finger.

And thus I leant against the wall, smoked, lingered
watched the Russendisko burp, and smoked
excessively. I was too bored to write.
Nevertheless not discontent. Wasted a thought
deciding not to leave this place just yet
when suddenly I saw this shirt, the ghost.

"O ghost," spake I, "forgive me, I was foolishly surprised.
Until you showed me I did not recognize
that ghosts appear in shirts and, rolling their eyes,
dispense comfort and discomfort counter- and clockwise."

The ghost just looked at me out of his shirt.
A girl came over asking for a light.
The man I was with wanted to go home.
I nodded like I didn't give a damn —

For a long time I'd been my own car crash,
my own sad gutted shell, hollow
my words clacked on like ghastly castanets,
vague and flimsy as smoke from a cigarette,
cold and precise as condensation.
I woke up in the tub as cold as ash.

Nonesuch II

I drew a bath and dreamed about those girls
that come up close and ask you for a light,
their little souls revolving in their eyes
in moments that my lighter will ignite.

And that is why I love these rituals
where they and I matchlessly unite
a little common interest. My cigarettes
are smooth and all exactly the same length. Thus

they prove that they and I are interchangeable,
pale, taciturn, bored and pretty unstable,
snapping and sighing when the fire's consumed
and in their youth full of desire, as breath
swings through their thicket, waking ghosts as well as
bundling artificial moments to their lips.

The ashes on the water form a cracking skin.
My darling, iff you vill be my giraffe,
I prommise to do zings to make you laugh.
The past has reached the level of my chin.
Ze beavers, dear, have gnawed off all ze trees
and as you look at me, zeir working on my knees.

The cock mutters a lullaby at my nape,
the water heater hums a deep and sullen bass.
I watch myself succumb to thickening solipsy,
soon brainmap's sleepy tentacles will cover me...

It makes no sense to sit here, not in this tub.
Time flies off the handle here in steam and suds.
I can't get you with animals or jokes, the water's running out,
the four AM ghost rises on the last gurgling bout.

N's Irony Junkyard II

In pink socks wobbly on Aida's bar
the waitress stands, her food chain blouse
no longer tucked, her arms are
tacking up garlands for mardi gras.

They used Ayrton Senna's name for ketchup.
"20% more content" reads the label
on all the empty buckets in the yard.
It isn't much once it has left the body.

We make dim jokes and we are serious.
We dim jokes with dim humour till they hurt.
We laugh about it, but we ask for more:
We want the Café Drechsler to be open.
We want more aphorisms from the pope.
We don't think resurrection's glamorous.

For Jesus Christ was only representing
what Happy-TV moderators are:
slim pickings of a joke that doesn't fly
although their barbers had encouraged them to try.

(I will cut people, not merely their heads.)
Whereas the Holy Ghost, like Sesame Street,
consists of nothing but a dusty studio
that tries to brighten up to cheer the janitor.

Who dreams tonight of pink socks on a bar?
The man who does the laundry every sunday
and gently helps her slip out of her perm
and asks: "What kind of slippers are you wearing?
I'm interested in all things orthopaedic!"
massaging her feet till she begins to cry.

An Induction to the Blues

> It's a very attractive little device that combines a frequency follower with a device that puts out harmony notes to what you're playing... Its main drawback is that the tone that comes out of it is somewhat like a Farfisa organ.
>
> —Frank Zappa on the Electro Wagnerian Emancipator

Elbows on turntable, there he stood,
I felt desolate, analogous,
as helplessly enfurrowed as a wax cylinder,
revolving sentimentally. Failing the dancefloor,

choliambic in the alcaic beats. Alcaic beats?
I hadn't reckoned on such subtle bass.
True, also hadn't looked over at the dj yet,
was only startled by the anacreontic mood.

The sight of him sent through me sighs and currents racing.
My heartbeat stopped by what looked so damn good.
He had me floored, and trampled by the dancers.
Vinyl was melting faster than molasses. Grooved by shock,
I dragged my carcass to the finish of the track.
Stayed within hearing. Will grounded, pounded slack.

He at the turntables could hardly keep
from knocking over his beer, his eyes from falling shut,
When he segued from one number to the next
it sounded like he was fighting against sleep.

(I thought perhaps at his day job he was unable
to shut out odious voices
pouring their problems on him through the cables
pounding his skull with all their petty noises.)

And after several more weary hours
- the club air gotten thick with odes –
my tired genius puts the final record on
and sits down next to me. His face solicits dialogue,
his mane hangs down and messes up my notes,
starts talking in his sleep – in horrible dialect.

Contingency and I

If something's possible, it's easy.
What might seem like a difficulty
is time. You love me or you love me not.
Then not. Perhaps you'll learn.

But if you learn, it's there or not.
No processes exist, just one/one/nought.
I sit down in the nought and don't understand.
Walk the line of the one to stop the unraveling.

We lumber clumsily in space and time.
If we learned anything, it is not to collide,
through trial and error.   I want more error.
The pop song, three minutes' pain, a flimsy vector,
remains digital. What is there to reveal?
One cheek or the other is immune.

Weren't we once analogue? Twas only interface,
sleepless among the inexplicable, and our tenses
flowed out of mathmachines, the unavoidable
shying away from understanding, the unhard world.

I touch you or I touch you not.
Between is compressed time,
unbalanced space, increasing poles,
nothing unfathomable, nothing without a name.

Ah, touch is not possible, I forgot.
Oh yes, we are all woven of the same
0/1 cloth, lifting and shoving.
Nothing must yield to anything, anything to nothing,
move swiftly, rad or hesitant,
backward, not liking, never loving.

translated by Ann Cotten and Rosmarie Waldrop

Ron Winkler

September Album

I

September, you say and gesture vaguely
toward the sky whose chameleon color
sways pale in the dusk.

open seams, I reply, my eye
on the sagging overland power lines
tipped with swallows waiting.

II

on a meadow gardeners comb up
the summer.

patiently. but too early, you object.

not all the herded bales of straw
had cleared the fields.

III

two days later it's fall. fog
massages the first frost off
the front of the land.

you say, you could tell my headache
from my limbs. I keep silent
preoccupied.

the night after, without a word you take
a handful of august out of your pocket.

IV

sunny days at this time
form rare lakes. Indian summer moths
there draw their circles. your voice
gives them airs.

V

a few sounds were still lacking,
you said, gliders, windjammers,
laundry drying on balconies and
the racket of a fleeing hare,
as well as — surely I knew —
the spiny gainsay of its hedgehog.

VI

when the fall storms start, you say,
they leaf through trees as if in search
of something. blacklegs perhaps, I smile,
in local one of the foliage union.

VII

even quince fall prey
to your eyes, playthings
for the lips below:
passable their attempt
to imitate
the midsummer sun.
your pity for them
as fuzzy as their corona.

VIII

said it was time now
to keep the last calendar leaves
to oneself and turn them
into quais, so the
imagined river
would not get lost.

IX

there were after all places that are nothing
but signifiers. almost unauthorized
in their own story. the sea for example:
a worn-down carpet. blindly
the waves were scouring the beach
for bathing nudes. in vain,
but hardly regrettable.

X

the blues of winter? —
a troupe of poplars wanders along the river
toward the next month.

for Petra Lang

surrounding Schnee

we love this cold fractal grammar.

the fine-boned tumble of snow through the air.

the complex prancing of fine-boned snow through the atmosphere.

the new territory in front of the *white boxes* of our eyes.
that simplifies the surroundings.

we love these soundless hooves of the beginning
of *it's snowing*.

we love these complicated intensive care units
of this particular climate.

their unobtrusive complexity.

the vividness of *specific unbalance*.

we love the turbulence that is its own proof.

and the phenomenon as such (as memory
of this phenomenon).

cautiously we love peaceful *overbombing*.

and later the creeping constructivism
of white sanscrit on things.

(for J.S., R.H. and M.R.)

the fact of rain

we consider the fragmented water as a phenomenon
between the adjectives *light* and *stormy.*

it never rained just once per rain.

sometimes we felt hormones navigating toward us.

sometimes: solid antonyms of *desert.*

we felt rain was the most drinkable weather.

as hydrogeneity.

it mostly rained away from the universe.

and toward the universe.

oceans swept over our heads. capsules
filled with themselves.

and the data of the first hour.

zoological waiting

future zero. it was a matter of gradual bio-organics in the form of
 contemplation.
afternoons like strange animals that snapped open their explainable eyes
 like equipment
or love. *present tense imperative passive.* that meant top utilization
and quickly prepared. sugar, placebo, and a bit of this psychic cargo.
past tense, respectively *downunder ligh*t. we gave each other freely
convertible grill software. locust raids. in any case complete things. *perfect:*
nano moments. teabag childhood. photos of remarkable junior staff: engineers
of filth that built circuits out of the integrated sand on the beach.
(Vita fragila). cacophonous wasps immediately conveyed to us their vivid
concept of a raging indicative.

pen insula

out of exaggerated dunes there gradually grew autumn.

we were there as Pollock weather hit us.

the waves — the sea was rough — fell back on any amount of water.

wet could break out at any moment.

fish we considered a strange kind of breath-content.

the bars of the grid of trees culminated in fruit.

other mobile containers looked like human beings.

that was only conditionally because of the outside.

souvenir trip

behind ample sheep lay premium highlands,
the alpha landscape immediately recognizable, the adequate
design tectonic middle class in its prime. you talked
of *mounting* together, a few egocentric pubs, later, of manic
harvest, who knows, these foreign parts were an intransitive
home — hence dangerous. malt cows were bred
that acted like malt cows. every day contained approximately
ten kilogram of beauty. sunrises like monsoons.
precipitation now like light, now nouns.
around us so-called Glenn-Gould-birds. strange windows.
they too were based on a charter language and bridged
something that was lacking. on leaving you gave them
a peculiarly victorian look.

for Jan Wagner

high-end-situation

morning alternated between delivering

atheism and hasty catholicizing.

the sun rays seemed modern. they refused

unambiguous messages. apropos:

behind some of these concepts I suspect trees.

in order to learn more I googled myself a walk —

through a rapidly subsiding forest.

not every ellipsis in it was a lake or pond. but almost.

en route, without meaning to, I stomped on the updates of some grasses.

they might have been beta versions.

the insolvent clouds in the sky had distracted

me.

organic garden

here the situations held out their nominatives to us.
avenues lined with casual trees (plantains). the lawn meant stagnation.
we were pleased, background-independent and evidently
accompanied by alleged bees with all their positive qualities.
the functions of other multicellular organisms wrung hyperlatives from us.
we had allowed for this. most beautiful the gentle dose of
doe motives at the edge of this park. *discrete portions* en route from
reality to the real.
and so helpfully helpless.

never the alps

what was more decisive for ascertaining mind: the
snow caribou
or
the caribou snow? the former looked like formally free haiku, the latter
like it.
from the milky overhang of the mountains avalanche
dogs came foaming down.
they were usable as objects (of communication). their eyes promised
discipline and valleys.
it was for their own safety that we recorded their biometric
data —
and established a subdomaine: *fur files*. this too was done
with Columbus methods.
the pastures to be valued most highly could almost
detach from
the concept of nature.
they were composed of clear definitions. these items
alone
were worth the trip.

for Steffen Popp

translated by Rosmarie Waldrop

Anja Utler

marsyas, encircled

> *Articulation also occasionally occurs [..] when inhaling (inverse sound). Thus, for example, an inverse [f] is used from time to time for the expression of a sudden, mild pain.* — R. Arnold / K. Hansen

much later is:
as if rattling as if: the breath got going and
along the edge capsules crackling, even cracking
the seeds they: spurt, spray deeper, back
from the shoreline, across the land

before that:
tongue lining the gums with whispers
chirruping, trilling in the (..) in the heat
lost in haze — fresh-cut grass — it's
whirring past — an echo — the wind

1

shaded — clasping

marsyas, it is: strung up on the tree trunk
soon: skinned, clawing the branch — pelt —
is: stretched, so shadows flee from the
axilla, being split by the blade
— breath spellbound — seeing: it opens up the dark
thoughts: streaming air and beaming light

—

so: groping, the fingers, they want to: scratch at the bark it: grates
    against the nails
it: breaks as though: loosened by light — [llh] — cracked, to the rind,
    the blindness below
— [ssp] — wood sprouting swelling up still deepening — in silence —
    the darkening heart

—

2

groping — remembered

—

only: rustling of: shoots the daphne's sprouting stalks, the:
buds redden early in the year: calyces sprung — so feverish,
it: bursts under the fingers — [ff] — quivering [fft] — feathery,
pierced by light, it: congeals to a bast-layer to stone-fruit

—

3

neatly: separating

him: to observe his: glistening limbs
slippery with sweat — spasms — whitish
by the tree: salt will flower from his armpit,
stiffen, crystallise, then when the skin's
shrunk by the wind, is parchment hanging
beside the scourged limbs — the flesh a cone

—

so: reeden the: leaf-spines spreading out from marshy soil: sedge
the sawgrass it: sways the conical corn-ears — [tss] — tips they
cut that cuts — [tsp] — whispers whispering through — the corneal
layer the fingerberries' buds — [fv] — carved: in the wind

—

4

rampant — pouring out

welted, bulges, fibres separated from the inside
hidden: that's how they wanted to germinate, the prickle-cells,
corneal cells: spraying layers, they wanted to surround
what should be called: cords to be counted, the: bones budding,
on the blades on: spiny outgrowths and
they'll need to be peeled off and: should the stomach muscles be
coupled with rhombodendron, trapezifoil, that lower, that raise the ribs
underneath: the lung, made tangible, (basically a bundle
beset by the pumping air

—

peeled: they are sharp-edged, leaves: in the panicled rib-stems such
trembling — [sst] — between the fingers on the flute's neck waving,
shuddering, they sever: split the airstream in two — [ssh] —
the rushes rustling the lips the panicles split, spilled: again into one

—

5

swirling — desolate

trembles — the air filled with fleeing birds, rustling sounds —
to finger the serrate's darkening furrows
pulling the stomach muscles — to see them: feathering fluttering
the ribs are: wings whirling and streaming there: the eyes mistaken
probe lost in a daze in a maze in shuddering (..)
ever more driven and scared: this gaping wound
the mouth: still deepening and silent
— a sudden karst — a parching plain

whilst:
is turned inside out: plunges — finally — toward him
and bursts forth gurgling shrieking — a groan —
and for now only he: marsyas is delivered from horror is —
lastly: he wells into the waiting land, has
no escape, he is the spring

                                                translated by Tony Frazer

sibyl — poem in eight syllables

> Sibyl: burnt out, sibyl: trunk.
> The birds extinct, but God appeared.
> —Marina Tvsetaeva

has: touched seeds, with the naked eye: naked mouth on
fire, sibyl, she shudders, flares: sand singes the tips the
fingers the tongue strikes sparks from the body: ablaze

•

she: staggers, sibyl, falls prey to: rippling sand she slips, streams
through her — a myriad pores — sweeps through her flickering the sun — turns:
sunstorm — she whispers, spits, she knows: it won't set again

•

is: burst, sibyl, the: splinter in the flesh is she — bleeding still? —
splitters — asunder, gapes: like lips, a stump — is: lamella, lignified
she: splits the light, soaked: shrills, it: wells up

•

sibyl thus: yawns, moans: vibrant the: vocal cords, the glottis, they
grate: across limestone, chafe, tear: crater from
pelvis to throat the: larynx, sibyl, she: trembles, throbs

•

throbs, is: the shaking, sibyl — the shock — winces: in whirling sand
and wind she gnashes rejects : the joint sprained, whines: to the
sand bar: pines away — shivers: uprooted pine — she: eroded

•

sibyl she: towers, turns into: cliffs she hisses is: spray in her
pores she smolders spatters: sibilants, expires -sss- ebbs
floods herself and: moans

•

she: sways dizzy, sibyl she: breaks in the whirling heat she: whispers
whirs: swamp, sump slippery thighs the: girdle of reeds wet she
entongues herself gurgles — adder — escapes and: chirrs

•

•

then quiet. only a scent of: scorched ground the clearing audible — the
former crackle — and rot: toes finger the stump:
a mushroomy hollow, poke at the molted skin: it crumbles
under the scaly soles and: a rustle

translated by Rosmarie Waldrop

Steffen Popp

Auratic Agrology

I

Imperceptibly cultivating a style, wind from the Northwest
and the garage door compose a flowing rectangle

the emotional project, strung out
it hangs before us, in the air, breathing laboriously

we seek to bind love's structures
in conversation, in the long forest-walks
through fog.

II

The heart foams heavily in its gazebo of pain
wild vines, screams, dry roses, silence

darkness spreads geometrically in quiet rows
in the island's hem of water lilies, floating pond scum
and forests are and
grounds, within which you vanish

the area, naturally artificial, correctly incubated
the loneliness of your mud boots, pragmatic
under your white knees

and in the evening can we not hear, behind the drunken roar
of lost witnesses, your swans in the biosphere, singing.

III

Always in shades of tiredness
snowed in, in mountains, in plains, in one's own body
to encounter — a
                    distant shore, overgrown with light,
        floating in self-invented fog . . .

odd correspondence with narcissi, saxifrage
this special technique of the sphere was called "living"
                                        "home"

instead we wanted to go deeper into the distilleries of tenderness
to never end this undistracted Yes

words, their sorrow, penguin tracks on the pack ice
to look at you walking, breathing—to contemplate
your childish fists in sleep . . .

IV

Speaking exhausts the community of pain
future settles on thought like a mold, like fire

in the rotunda, a red horse standing there, made from copper
the blood in your fingers, the party lights
ring the trees like a wilted piano.

To walk around, restless, striking a few keys
sometimes the music lures something out

the instant in the play of twigs
a longing, carved out of cheap stone lovers announce the night

cold fusion, centaur

whoever steps within range of trees is alone.

                                translated by Christian Hawkey

Bert Papenfuss

*two ethnographical poems
extracted from riddles of a Siberian tribe*

FATHERS AND SONS

In the dark yurt
a rotting boot rolls.
The moon is shining. The water is boiling.

From the middle
of the hot pond
bald heads rise up.
Ice freezes and melts.

A dappled horse
strikes the frozen mountain.
The jackdaw picks frozen dung.

While the father is wrapped in nappies,
the son rises to the sky.
Smoke from the hearth of the yurt.

On the handle of the knife
lies a town. Strokes,
fondles, scratches and chats.

With a stone sail a boat
rides suddenly over the Ob.
The mist sinks gradually.

In the bleak,
in the deserted wood
wanders a pair of leather pants.

In the bleak, in the deserted
wood redbeard stands in heaps.
Black grouse and agaric.

Along the edge of the meadow
warriors ride on a raft.
In the Irtysh the fish are rising.

Along the mountain
a band of warriors travels on foot.
The leaves are falling. The way grows shorter.

"Enemy advances, we retreat;
enemy halts, we interfere;
enemy grows tired, we strike;
enemy retreats, we pursue."

MOTHERS AND DAUGHTERS

On the roof of the yurt
eaten by horseflies
a huge reindeer fell. The stars.

A naked man,
the shirt clutched to his chest,
makes light. The spark flying.

A clever woman
threads pearls on a string.
A squadron of geese takes off.

A nasty animal
in the bridle of twenty
to thirty. Tongue and teeth.

Between the houses
bloody lumps of meat being carried
around. Gossip and malice.

Has no hand,
has no foot, climbs
higher. The dough rising.

Four women,
a cloth round them.
The table is laid.

The thunder cracks,
a Russian glove
is thrown, a child being suckled.

A good horse brings
the night with a sling.
The spindle at the end of the thread.

In a corner of the bleak,
of the deserted wood a woman
is crying under a red headcloth. Fungi.

In the middle of the village
a knotty burr stands.
The church. A squirrel's nest.

"The yellow crane has gone, who knows where?
Lingers only the wanderer's rest.
Wine offered to the rippling river,
the stream of the heart swells high with the waves."

from *Rumbalotte continua*

BRAVADO

I was Cathar and Bogumil,
Bogislaw, Bogoljub and Kolup,
Albigensian and Waldensian,
Publican and urban savage,
Geopoliticist, Selenopolite,
heliopolitan, cosmopolitan,
Zenithist[1] and hajduk-comitadji.[2]
lurker in the offing and share and share alike pirate
my fellows were
        "the accursed and scapegrace folk,
        imps of the sackless devil,
        the Victalian Brethren."[3]
I was a peasant rising up, a voidoid like Richard Hell,
Anabaptist and Kuhlmannian,
satanist and freemason,
stower and stevedore,
mutualist and egoist,
narodnik and nihilist,
rigorist, blanquist, terrorist,
social revolutionary, maximalist,
ultra-universalist and nabatist,
in short social democrat and socialist,
which falls heavily off the tongue —
well, I was an aramcheckist too;
I am sorry to say I regret nothing.
My fellows are irregular,
of accelerated mobility,
antipolitical engagement
and maritime cockiness.
I am a communist, an anarchist,
arachnist, sinister radical —
and already worked up.

        Shramm-sharam
        experience outcomes!
        Shramm-sharam
        come out with experiences!
        The time for words is past!

I brought the cargoes at intervals,
fetched the booty in crises,
fought in battles, the planned sort,
and the ones accepted with no plan,
dead earnest and laughable —
till they fell out of their skins,
I plundered freebooters,
ravaged armies, hid fences,
committed the greatest errors,
in the gravest emergencies
put cowards in my pockets;
cowards longing for gelt
in pockets steering for hell.
"The storm is roaring
the house is cracking —
we want to break violence
by means of violence..."[4]

        Klatsch-kalatsch,
        as I lay me down,
        klatch-kalatch-nikov,
        that's how I get mine, Ulyanov.
        The time for words is past!

In stripes or checked
I was never correct,
snagged up everywhere;
as Syrdon implosively fucked
the virtuous Soslan on his kneecaps,
as Loptr, always on the slant,
on-heat and deception set aside,
I sent Baldur a-wooing
to the old never to be seen again,
we all find our way to hell sometime.
        "My name is Arrivederci
        I bring greetings from my
        big brother the raven
        Nevermore"[5]
I was a piss mystic, missing from muster,
sore thumb, lyric poet,
weakling, sad sack, muscle man,
megalo, tosspot and endurance fighter,
ugly bird, empiricist,
fantasist, bringer,

silent man, demonstrator;
never a soldier, never a mercenary —
and in the final analysis once again
without qualifications a bag of noise:
a loud word
that leaves hearts stirred
goes on being heard

> shvam-shavam
> shavarma; by the cods of Bodhidharma,
> shvam-shavam,
> make way there for my karma.
> The time for words is past!

I am against every nation,
hate stadium and television,
competition, mangers and animals being fed,
baptism mass or individual,
masses in the streets and factories closed one by one —
knee on the chest,
cunning behind the ears
the rascal looks out —
on top of that all the Isms
along with their acolyte schisms,
I hate the unit, the army
east and west, the air force and the navy,
all I say is: RUMBALOTTE!
On my way downwards I am nimble,
stop for no barriers, wave at no full trains,
leave no window alone and don't let any door be closed,[6]
to property I prefer what's socialistic,
and to the economy the shadow economy,
to communication directness,
to linguistic expression the pre-modern kind,
mouldering in spelling reforms,
what the whole barrack understands, but
> "All deductions
> from the old language structure
> cannot yet be drawn
> because the right perceptions often miss us.
> Diversions are hard to avoid.
> To make material living
> remains a daring feat, and yet
> we are only concerned with the living"[7] however —

> Shlam-shalam,
> the ranks have been thinned,
> shlam-shalam,
> now the soundproofing is coming out.
> So the time for words is past?

Intervention, veto! Art is a weapon —
in times of peace, but at present, so long as prostitutes are in power i.e.
anyone at all is in power —
> I am against every government
> and any staging of events —
so long as art is the weapon,
put up resistance and shoot back.
> For bravado
> is the real double barrel —
however without precision
the astronomy shifts around
cracks your glasses
and goes down the wrong pipe
like Josef Vissarionovich's
administrative intervention
in linguistic prole-matics
leads straight to the labour camp.
> "[...] to eradicate the existing language
> constructing instead a new language
> in the course of a few years
> would that not introduce anarchy
> into social life, would it not
> call into being a serious danger
> of a breakdown of social life?
> Who except Don Quixote
> could pick up this task?"[8]
Well, Don Quixote, Rumbalotte continua,
Lothar Feix, Rex Joswig, Brasch, Barbasch,
Barabbas, Coca-Carola and Roccococooler,
> "Sitting, laughing
> at the mindless humanoids
> croaking in their swarm.
> While recalling Omar Khayyam."[9]
Young Cuchulainn, old Jemtschik,
Kling the smooth, the wrinkled Dring,
a few more dissidents and I
will get the language rocking.
Among the arses a battering ram is prince.

And you "Well now, you redhead, [...]
better come with us,
we're going to [Port Watson
and for all I care to Bremen too]
something better than the [State]
you can find anywhere;
you have a good voice,
and when we make music together,
it's going to be a special sound."[10]

Brasch-barasch, Barbasch,
Barabbas; from out of the ground,
out of the mist the barrel rises up —
and goes to the balls, doh.
The time for words is past-a-past.

However it was discussed
 it went the way of Ate-te.
Too much naked skin on show,
in the words of Eastrock:
a game too slow for the hunter
the comb sticks on the back of the throat.
Knicker elastic, benzene chains,
Anarchy is stuck in change.
70s sleaze,
80s sleaze,
90s sleaze
3000 years sleaze
gives us entertainment,
pays the administration.
Joyful fertility, scabby curves
gives us entertainment,
little tits kindly request,
pay the administration
Knicker elastic, benzene chains,
Anarchy is on the change.

The young people of today
are a divided mob.
> "Stupidity expresses itself everywhere
> when an individual draws
> out of his life and attitude towards his environment
> conclusions for himself and others
> for which he has no other proofs than himself.

[...] In daily life this means when someone believes
what is not so, when someone demands
that others should believe it,
because he already believes it, and because it's more secure
when many believe than when one does and finally
when all these people then make a law of
believing what isn't so,
just so that stability isn't threatened.
[...] This is how it is with the capitalist system
and the state which is built upon it."[11]

Piss squirter, sensitive spirit, Afro-Amestigon!
When the film tears on Amalthea,
broadcast Albemuth off where no pig can defecate.
Survival is not some kind of song.
The time for words is past-a-past-a-past.

Kosher slaughter the media, bleed them out,
the logistics of dazzle
finds employment elsewhere.
Attack advertising, raze west Hungary—
a little joke on the stroll,
if the rhyme is always impure,
if we ride into disaster,
of course I don't mean West Hungary,
but the reactionary Kuomintang!
Shit on the rich range of parties
property owners have no right to speak;
use footballers, actors
and jugglers and other
puppets and string pullers of
the military-industrial complex
to wipe yourselves clean with!
Stability of classes is an abuse.
        In every game there are
        heroes, losers and winners,
        even in earnest there are
        heroes, losers and winners.
        The winner is broken on the wheel,
        the loser climbs the scaffold,
        and the hero up the Enchanted Rubble Mountain,
        where more than earthly pleasures await him
        with the underground beings.
        His occasional trips outdoors

      are seen as returns of the dead.
      In gulps the witnesses
      recover from the shock.

Drink reformists and revisionists under the table
and ship the piss out — to Denmark,
perhaps a cow can benefit. Learn Danish,
Swedish, Finnish, Russian, Estonian,
Latvian, Lithuanian, Polish, Czech,
French, Belgian-Boeotian and tinkers' cant.
Shabby, shameful and infamous
is the daily struggle to be on top.
Banish the servants of the state,
renounce chucking names of plants and animals
along with compost and carrion abusives
at rascals and leavings —
any old shit is useful
for something in the end.
Correct the gender!
respect every species!
Rotate on the spit
with all the force of the counter-culture
and the armed blues
of the counter-continental movement.
 Wind on the general clock,
declare the general clearout!
"So anarchy runs
              homeless
in vitalistic-idealistic rambling,"[12]
yet sharing the knowledge of the detective
about the appropriation of economic material
after the overthrow words will follow deeds.

           "It's my fault...
           and it's your fault." That's over!
           "Where we are not, are our enemies..."[13] That's over!
           The time for words is beginning again!

NOTES:
Rumbalotte: from a joke about a seaman who has tattoos everywhere including his cock. The joke involves the word "Rumbalotte" which under other circumstances expands to read "Ruhm und Ehre der baltischen Flotte" (glory and honour of the Baltic fleet). The Baltic fleet is significant to Papenfuss as he comes from Pomerania and identifies with the Communist sailors of the Baltic Fleet near St Petersburg. "Rumbalotte" is also a sailing ship which won a world championship race in 1968. There was however a dance number called "rumbalotte" (related to the rumba?). "Lotta continua" was an Italian revolutionary group of the 1980s.
Papenfuss' volume of poems 1998-2002 was called *Rumbalotte*, however this poem is from the sequel, *Rumbalotte continua*, and there is a third series of poems under this title.

Notes on sources:
1. Zenitism: avant garde movement founded by Ljubomir Micic in Zagreb in 1921. See 'Manifesto of Zenitism' in W. Asholt/ W. Fahnders, *Manifeste und Proklamationen der europaischen Avantgarde (1909-1938)*, Verlag J.B. Meltzer, Stuttgart/Weimar, 1995
2. from the manifesto *Manifesto to the barbarians of the spirit and thought on all continents*, by Ljubomir Micic, 1925: "We roar from the age old cradle of culture. We of the Balkans roar anti-culture!... anti-Europe! We want to avenge ourselves like men, eye for eye, tooth for tooth! Today we fight with rebel poems, for our calling is: Poet-rebel, haiduk-comitadji."
3. 1549 Plattdeutsch chronicle by Reimar Kock
4. The storm: quote from Karl Plattner, *Organised Red Terror*.
5. quote from Karl Mickel, *Geisterstunde*.
6. from Andreas Koziol, *If only we had remained a utopia*, 2001
7. Ernst Fuhrmann (1931)
8. from *Marxism and Questions of Linguistics*, J.V. Stalin, and N. Marr, "On the origin of language."
9. from *Roccocooler,* The Edgar Broughton Band 1973
10. from "The Bremen town musicians," a Grimms tale
11. from an article in *Der Gegner*, Berlin 1924, author probably Franz Jung.
12. Ernst Bloch, *Freedom and Order.*
13. from the film, *Berlin — Ecke Schonhauser*, DEFA 1957

Amestigon: name of a demon in a tale by Alexander Kuprin.
Selenopolis: city on the moon in various SF stories, such as Star Trek.
Albemuth: reference to novel by Philip K Dick (*Radio Free Albemuth*).
Aramcheck are a government-run underground opposition in the same novel.

translated by Andrew Duncan

Uljana Wolf

forest master rod
shakespeare titus andronicus

I

> *the woods are ruthless, dreadful, deaf, and dull*
> titus, act 2, scene 1

in woods in woods the mosslit paths
horny and lined with bloodlines

plotted with the buried drives there
called victory and roman honorandglory

and did i mention dark mention fear
and scoundrel hour of two brothers that

were called demetrius and chiron: sons
of tamora anti-romans sleazy balls of

history their goth-gonads antithetically
jacked up for the hunt—in the woods

there in woods they unleashed vengeance
their dicks printing a message on the moss

II

as from a conduit with three issuing spouts
titus, act 2, scene 4

don't say rome and roe don't say dainty doe
say hunting not pluck a rose plow a field

not plunder flower beds or bed not judge
but simply flee into *wasserkunst*: to pull

the plug on this commandless speech this
treacherous stutter-trough which spills

red the legend lavinia that you are and are
not oh conduit with three issuing spouts speak

darkly a word goes down the drain and dark
with blazon and blahblah from the fountain's

floodmouth blundering now and blind i greet
a later i your reader your repeat offender

III

thou map of woe, that thus dost talk in signs
titus, act 3, scene 3

the father speaks: you map of woe you
cipher folded thrice and net enmeshed

in the markings of the messengers how
shall i unfold or read or speak for you

if not of my own pain—you are missing
a hand so i will let mine fall or have it

felled and if i knew they`d dug a grave
between your thighs (i didn't realize until

act 4, scene 1) i would submit my ass instead
to aaron's führer rod let my own folds

cramp and tatter into illegibility the
bodies i say are the fly heads of rome

IV

> *faint-hearted boy, arise, and look upon her*
> *titus, act 3, scene 1*

we read what we saw picking up with
our eyes open from the blank lens—

woods' edge muddy hem foaming lids
we did not see the center the scene

unseen behind a curtain of thick limbs
which spewed you now onto the screen:

a heap of signs a slash and stab fest in
the tongue-root routine the bodies of

daughters flawlessly cut up in ovidian
design lacerations we saw you lavinia

in a live stream we read and in all eyes
you were the cataract the horror star

translated by Christian Hawkey

Christian Hawkey / Uljana Wolf

Erasures

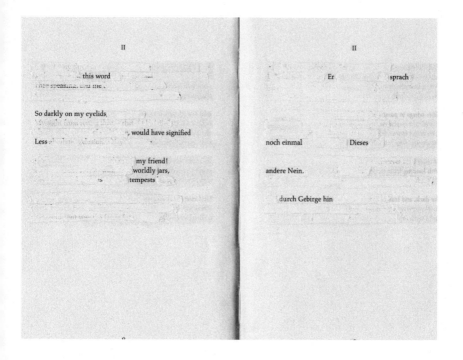

III

O

wings in passing.

What hast *thou* to do
With looking .
through

The dark, and leaning up

III

Glänzender
dein Auge

gräbt solches um

IV

The dancers
watching

here unaware
at my door?

The bats and owlets

in further proof
aloof.

IV

Du bist da

und deinem Mund

gefällt diese dürftige Tür
in goldnen Falten

die
Eule

Das Echo   das Haus,

V

As once Electra

                lay hid in me,
the red wild

beside me

The hair beneath.

V

         Auge schau
         Asche

                      schau

an meiner Seite warte t

Feuer   dein Haar

VII

        the footsteps
             as they stole

  a new rhythm

The names   are changed

      are only
          what they say.

VII

      das   gesicht
in einem andern

         ner Rhythmus

               bist du

wo du bist   ein Ort
      (die Engel wissen wie

X

when I   need
love

Out of my face
       the   meanest creatures

       doth flash

X

                    ist sie nicht
schön

verwandelt

über dem Dunkeln, das ich bin: ich seh,

XIII

                  the winds are rough,
Between our

             feet

XIII

            Beweise
Liebe

            alles war

                 mein   Kleid

Hendrik Jackson

Seam. (Hölderlin-Cut)

Strange these many leaves here: narrow, thin
and so green. Beginning of winter, much sun.

Her nineteen-year-old face fitting. A
bucket of icewater ready, your face, your head — in with it.

The most unraveled nearness *(mountains, O give us)* — a lie
sewn alongside with a few stitches. Inflicted, fugue.

starless

Unmoved usefulness of lanterns at the town exit
    a surface slides into the road: -always-
        so-cold-draft; *(sleeves sleeves)*

Standing there marveling *(no omens)* at blackness
    this total absorption: outside -still-
        growing staffs; *(delete, soundless)*

On the sea-surfaces of the universe a psalm's unrolling overtones
    I grasp and grasp, it moves upward: -lightless-
        hanging glacier ice; *(now, haptic)*

Deleuze/Bergson

I
time climbed into closure
on a thread while we

on puppet wire in back
casually changed positions

icewater in the dark — a face
to other solar systems tied

II
On impact the train jolted
the rails into a loop —

layer by layer it replayed
in ghostly circles of recall;

a negligeable moment
and the memory of the world.

brackets

as if for the last time (the final) embrace
       the expanded boundaries
the oblique whispers: a shadow must I
       have wished to be.
then these pictures, fine cuts interleaved,
       tiny lamellae,
if i blink i see sprouting there
       a space of death.

Life in Buried Rooms

Nightly hum –hovering– and among *(twisted, apostrophied)* loops
the announcement: always describe the same radius *(life in buried rooms)*.
Evening climbed iron poles, beyond them more cumbrous ruins.
Though doubly made up for with burden and love — speaking was still
    a kind of loss,
Bodies bent over with time *(a switch)* — numb forearm *(Persephone's bees)*
in a shadowy world: gestures *(silence, gaps)* and warm animal eyes that deceive.

Freiburg

Eyes — closed *(ah little veins)*, ghostly afterimages remains.
(Memory) follows forgetting — just as blindness comes
before seeing — cat eyes *(slits, lazy)* blinking — the black drafty room
turns into woods *(moss)* a branch a call a worthy steeple dream.

Picture postcards to sing in rhythm –merrily-o– by the big door
st.george-boots *(sneakers)*, ah *(proud-lashed)* Marina: on horseback *(death)*, I hear
already the clatter *(armament cash)*, hinged visor: so through brooks the
    images stream,
white shirt *(like larks)* and asphalt, stands still my hero with shield and spear.

"in a fog…" *(Hesse)* — backward: life: a poet's sleep, comes bowling a ball.
We pay. Doors slam *(and)* slowing plash *(with night in our arms)* we talk
— how long we walked *(woods) (woolly hair)*: now façades in stone;
O how scattered: the waves and signals — a crystal grows in air unseen.

Return of the dead *(till we fall asleep)* — overflow *(in the)* dark:
branched space of years: or splinters short *(and maybe too:)* from other times.

Crossings (Tram Lines, Frequencies)

Poles, cables, passers-by. Wave after wave, gone.
(Behind you a high year). Manes, streams, lines of cars — Still
A bit of a boost. A park. Self-conscious — put a gruffness on
Your words. Head in the grass — how all tones wove into one:

Seven marked high on the back, bright hue of hands — palms—
Her cheek, steel grazed it *(pressed her back against the cool)*
Where she was was near *(or more distant still)* duino *(blue)*
laughs; pulse, light signals *(gentle gliding)*, newly soft — relaxed —

Morse code, invisible, just lines: possible: folds, waves.
All drowned out, droning all round –closed eyes– the light dead.
Just audible: a gentle plashing *(distant)* as in the first summer-bright
night… as tenderness *(drag)* weaves its one black thread.

TORN OPEN the blue in the sky, dark streak, the string of an eyepatch.
A slight gust among papers, blinking a sheet sails from the *(half-near)* satchel.

On the paved banks: blackbird *(trill, shift, roll)*, a valley enclosed.
The cube turns *(time):* new figure, the movement slows.

Sideways *(drawn)* streaks *(on the trees)*, schlieren in the sky.
Summer bloom, body-drunk, greedy, dropping joints *(barques – gone by)*.

Squalls over the pavement — back — sail — an island, blinks in the dark.
Don't let go, word for word *(over pages)* returns *(at length)* there,

fern, thicket, the empty ever-blooming valley, soft moss, *(barques–
gone by)* Eleonore — a tiny pulsing vein –so distant– laid bare.

translated by Rosmarie Waldrop

Franz Josef Czernin

the mouse (a feat)

if the finger
that points at the lion
wears a ring
that he jumps through,
the sign multiplies the beasts
in the name of our whole shebang
—not just for the sake of the males.

oh fine courage,
queen between bulging bars,
such a hole
is filed by the cat
on such a chain
howls the dog
that link by link
eats his own tail.

tigerpaper

from the rubble of all foam
such a spray of scraps
rises the lion of significance,
shakes his mane
— plants, words, happiness — and
serenely, in the full splendor of fear,
with the full weight of fury,
roars, pisses and fucks
(gull to his own best performance),
crumples sparkling into his prey,
spits about what good he does,
and finally cuts
— lamb in his own understanding —
himself in stripes and with this
sentence bursts in all directions

oar

yes, for the sake of parting
heavy with so much ore
and very much on a thread
yet more above my neck
the sword cut into the sea:
where does the sea lie on its roar?

no, to alleviate pain
what took the umbrella to the rain
and curved the worm to its ways,
and from of so many blank spots
and toward my fishing pole
a pigeon wants to carry his mail:
what does the fish cuttle in this ink?

what does a snake stream in paper?
as to as fro with all these turns
perhaps, too, with a wise man's goal
the screw's afraid of rust,
the hand grabs at its own petard:
how does this marmo set and that mar mot?
and does the nail its head feel not?

proceeds. (rent)

later then the night stands by
the night, circles black
as blight, resplendent
as eight kites in flight
and broke as darkness
the trend toward sight, accent
and accident and did not mention bent
and had not broken any
sound from any fright
or had already squandered
any pay and shot
its wad on a Chev-
rolet.

from: *oral work-out and piglatin*

> when the eyes fall shut
> the door opens up,
> comes a beast and
> gives you a look.

1

who is not his own whirlwind?
what cowboy doesn't ride his favorite tune
back home and what is home but
a weather forecast never true?
and if you claim that such a traveler
must face preparing his last words
you could be wrong.

high winds, whirlwinds all round the earth!
even the compass rose turns with the wind
only as it is plucked,
and that the weathercock's wild feathers
must coax his bloodred comb
to comb the last ray out of evening
won't keep poor homesick hens
from laying eggs as round as balls
even if you ask in your sleep
why everything keeps going on.

because all turns but around itself!
hardboiled or softboiled makes
no diff however small.
if you sing to nostalgia of mother sun
you end up without horse flat on your nose.
but what does all this have to do with your tongue
that curls to look in your heart?

2

the trees that leaf through everything,
mountains that have nothing to do
with climbers,
and the wide wide world is
what nobody has yet seen
with an open and dry eye.
for an open and dry eye's
not armed with organs of the sea.

but I, and this makes waves,
have been in water
if you've been in water
over both your ears you'll tilt
your ear and shake your head
to be rid of it
and never mind the deaf and blind.

no we don't need to bother with
the history of captains
to claim certain enemies:
your own head strikes out on its own
and tears its hair while
the ground starts to give from the ground up
with absolute pokerface.

yes I've been in water, and the waves
that got in my eyes and ears
have plunged my several bodies into
a gale of washed-out laughs.
it didn't go so far that
my whole head left my neck.
still it's with great caution i looked
across the bank into the lake:
and right into the eye
of a distinctly unfamiliar guy.

3

the dot on the i, of this i say nothing!
a pointing finger shows, grows and has
finished its tune. i must, you fuss:
it's the same old song, i.e. a father
with guts for a totally in-house concert.
a hand makes a fist, a child's asleep
cool butter. open window, behind: nothing
to throw out of this spic-and-span town.

finishing touch: sweep it between your temples
so your fingers can stretch into pure air.
finally cause for applause from the heart!
gentleman mushroom and ladyslipper face a single gardener.
where is it, the trace that's lost in the distance?
an open window, but ah, you don't know
that my song's long gone over hills and away.

dog, cat, horse and hen, and all domestic animals!
stay simple and in your own bod: wind in the trees
makes no less of a roar than the fine big ocean,
in stray wall flowers blooms eternal snow.
the dot on the i is what i can't say,
the whole land dumps collection plates on me:
but the hand withers, fingers fall off,
windows flap their wings til not anything goes.

*4 meaningful and monotonous sonnets
from the fall of ~~19~~ nineteenhundredeighty*

                how it can happen or rather not happen that we can
                (not) see or rather (not) experience

                the leaf for the leaves
                   the leaves for the leaf
                      the leaf for the foliage
                        the foliage for the leaf
                          the leaves for the foliage
                            the foliage for the leaves

                as well as: the tree for the trees
                       the trees for the tree
                        the tree for the forest
                          the forest for the tree
                            the trees for the forest
                              the forest for the trees

he who plants trees inside a tree
  plants forests in mid-forest,
    he who plants leaves outside a leaf
      makes the leaf prosper without foliage

        he who drives out one of the trees
          drives this forest out of all forests
            but he who drives leaf after leaf into leaves
              makes leafless leaves and foliage grow

                he who finally — in the face of forests, trees
                  (and under leaves) instead of one tree after another
                    plants only this one plant bereaves the tree of trees

                      and pulls what otherwise in trees and forests blooms
                        into this leaf which — by not branching into other
                          leaves — bereaves the leaf of leaves

that this tree in those trees florishes
 crosses this leaf with leaves that here
  this twig growing over there
   pulls and drives into twigs, just as

     the branch that, branching here and there,
      branches into such other branches
       that the root — reproducing from here
        from there — also grows roots elsewhere:

         where every forest with all forests, name-
          ly forest after forest grows into one growth where
           tree and trees, leaf and leaves and twigs

            and branch and branches, forest and forests
             — in short anything florishing anywhere —
              are planted as plants that are the same.

as variation on the preceding sonnet:
a sonnet staggering with the effort at meaning

that this tree also in others florishes
 crosses this leaf with leaves because here
  this tree — leaves growing over there —
   drives sap into the twigs, just as

     the branch that, branching here and there,
      branches into such others: branches
       that the root — reproducing from here
        from there — grows its roots elsewhere:

         where every forest with all forests, name-
          ly the forest of forests grows into one growth which plants
           tree and trees, leaf and leaves and branch

            and twigs, branches, and forest, forests
             — in short anything florishing anywhere —
              as the plants that stand for everything though they are the same.

from this leaf here and this leaf there will no —
no, no foliage will from such leaves bloom;
   likewise the twig here and the twig there will not
   draw boughs from two grown twigs.

   from the branch here and the branch there will no —
   no, no ramification will for such branches bloom;
      likewise the tree here and the tree there will not
      draw a whole forest from two grown trees:

      and for the forests here, the forests there
      will there a third one come about for both?
         could leaf and twig and branch and tree that are here,

         and leaf and twig and branch and tree that are gone
         as foliage, boughs, ramification and forest, no,
         not for one another somehow bloom?

                          translated by Rosmarie Waldrop

Margret Kreidl

from *Noisy Pairs*

HIGH STAKE KNIVES

In the beginning was the dining sword.
You've cut your meat now eat.
The vegetarian slaughters the Welsh rabbit.
A knife in hand is better
than two chops in the frig.
One knife whets the other.
A cutlass to spite your prick.
A saber is a male child.
Veterans wear honorary dagger mock-ups.
Americans call bayonets theater props.
A Swiss army knife may save your life.
Holbein knives are most rare.
Whole bone daggers, museum exhibits.
A child's sword to cut his teeth.
Beheading machine, ten letters.
A switchblade triggered by light.
Not all knives cut a caper.
A wife's knife to carve a mistress.
A baker's dessert knife — doughboys' despair.
Catholics massticate instead.
The pro blade is fine stainless steel,
the beloved's cut, silk and chenille.
The Maestro's fork forks anywhere,
his knife cuts only camembert.
Knife fork scissors steel make a child a bloody meal.
The more knives the worse the company.
A knife in the cream gives you bad dreams.
Victorious soldier, a knife in his back as chaser.
Blackmail comes with a paper knife trail.
A paring knife for the au pair.
A writer's best blade: the eraser.

ADAM AND EVE

What do ladies wear? asks Adam. Eve is naked.
Fringed scarf? Pleated taffeta skirt? Too proper, laughs Eve.
Patent leather G-string fishnets transparent mini.
Adam giggles, Tops! High heels with ankle straps.
Don't forget shaving the legs. Wax or cream?
Hot, hot, cries Adam. Eve softly: ladies suffer.
Adam weeps. Eve smiles. Tears make ugly.
Foundation powder rouge. Kissproof lipstick.
Adam wants to smooch. Think of your hairdo. Hair
to tease nails to polish. Eve contented: very feminine.
Adam minces to the mirror. Eve is naked. Sit down Adam.
Now let's practice sitting standing walking. Spread your
legs a bit. And smile Adam smile. Get up stand still.
Not so stiffly. And walk. Naked Eve walks up and down.
This way. Head up and chest out. I want such big apples
too. Hands off! Adam gropes Eve's fig. No!
It's my fig. Adam cries: I want one too.
If you like, smiles Eve. Snip snip tail clipped.
Thank God, laughs Adam. Now I'm a lady.

SUMMER PARADISE

Wild romantic mountain panorama beach with
privacy aquapark thermal garden tropical bar
hamam nightclub program Greek evening grilled
lamb and sangria mediterranean climate hermitages
in island style water gymnastics digital massage attractive
diving base active volcano landscape with lava sculptures
acupuncture and algae therapy amphitheater sacrificial altar
of Aphrodite professional cooking class tastefully decorated
motto buffet Neptune grotto sundeck with internet corner
children's pool miniclub Cinderella relax center medicinal
cosmetics stepp-aerobics disco casino with
Byzantine frescos recently restored Minoan
labyrinth welcome-drink German language tours
fishing village with typical sand dunes bargain days in April
private tip resting pool in the pine forest early bird discount
idyllic summer paradise

VOYAGE ON FISHBACK
           after an oil painting by Max Beckmann

Sunset on Sochi. A street with blooming
acacia. The old Bolsheviks sing in chorus. Red
pigeons fly up. Where? Whence? Tamara de Lempicka! Whereto?
To Crimea. Sevastopol. Women in black are fishing on the
harbor walk. A Russian bride builds a castle in the air
on the gold coast. Midnight in Varna. The moon high
on the edge of the painting. Corona borealis is the name of
Thetis's crown. Crete. Tourists photograph the chained minotaur.
Tamara de Lempicka paints a green dolphin. Tripoli,
Bay of Tunis. Near Carthage bathes a barbarian Venus.
American sailors fuck under palms. Balearic islands, Costa
Brava. Tamara de Lempicka enjoys her fishback voyage.
Nice in sight!

HE AND SHE

My tender buttercup
My gentle goldenrod
My proud morning-glory
My pearly mayflower
My sparkling jewelweed
My fragrant lady's-slipper
My hot pussytoes
My wild Dutchman's-breeches
My hairy honeysuckle
My prim rose

You peroxide alcove-apollo you
You provincial pebbledrill you
You creepy billygoat you
You sad mouse-milker you
You perverse cowlicker you
You ludicrous wagtail-chaser you
You randy penny-pisser you
You lecherous tree-climber you
You effeminate wind-whipper you
You lefthanded snotrag-carrier you

ILSA AND LISA

Penis-defizit. Ilsa indulges in fantasies. Traumatic cut.
I am castrated. Lisa giggles. Ilsa, frustrated: ego-formation
is important. Lisa masturbates. Ideal-ego Ego-ideal? Lisa
laughs. No matter. Jujube jam jar. Honey flows. Lisa enjoys
narcissistically. Ilsa projects: The image is me. Ilsa is Lisa's
mirror. Things burst. Lisa grins: prickling nipple
teasers? Ilsa's impulse-ego gows dense. Giant
glitter dildo? Ilsa is happy. Ticklefinger lipthriller?
Impulse-aim furrow fissure. Ilsa jubilates: libido fluctuates.
Fresh crevice. Pleasure principle. Fi. Lisa spits. Ilsa fishes. Bi- or what?
Lisa does without: sublimation's the right thing. Ilsa commands:
Lust-ego! you love me. Lisa does not react. Ilsa regresses,
oral-sadistic. Impulse-fate? Lisa is sweating. Clitoris principle.
Lisa trembles. Ilsa eats Lisa.

SWEET PARADISE

Punch doughnuts potted cheese. What fragrance! Nut wafers
kipferl crescents nutballs nougat tongues. Open your mouth!
Linzertorte suger plums. A dream! Zabaglione
wine cream. So feathery! Chocolate soufflé coffee parfait
strawberry jellly. Ilsa feasts. Floating islands cockaigne strips
vanilla divinity. Ilsa regales herself. Meringue velvet. How delicious!
Almond fudge plum tart. Yeast omelet. So opulent.
Charlotte Malakoff. Ilsa gluts. Poppyseed braids apple crisp
coeur a la crème. This is tops! Salzburger Nockerl.
Mocha croissants. One more! Bûche de noël. Ilsa is happy.
Royal velvet rum chiffon pie baba au rhum. Ilsa smacks her lips.
Blueberry blintzes. Yummy! Nesserode pie.
Ilsa groans. Yeast dumplings. Ilsa pants. Puff paste
Nut wafers. Ilsa sighs. Cherry bavarian. Streusel cake.
Enough! Zuppa inglese chocolate mousse coconut macaroons. No more!
Ilsa swallows. Baked alaska hasty pudding. Ilsa munches.
Apple turnovers cream cheese piroges. Latkes halushka
Ilsa snorts. Rice Romanoff joan-at-the-stake
peasant pig's ears apple strudel. Ilsa grunts. Cheese strudel
Marzipan frangipan. No more! Chocolate kisses vermouth macedoine
strawberries nino gingered figs pears helene. Ilsa sweats.
Pears bordelaise plum popovers. Ilsa bursts. Batzerlguglhupf.

PEACH AND BANANA
after a collage of Max Ernst

The psyche is cracked. Madame sees herself in the mirror
with beard and fur. O great St. Uncumber! The bedroom's not
for shaving. Madame says a depilation prayer.
Please, thank you and amen. A peach lies in bed. Total
hairloss. Banana. Amor has an erection. Love parade?
The banana has a red peel. Madame shows her parts
of velvet and silk. The bow is drawn. The peach smells
sweet. O wonderous depilation! Amor kneels down
and kisses the bare calves of his lady. The banana grows.
The peach falls out of bed. An arrow flies across the room.
O holy bearded Uncumber! Madame stands on her head. Navel
kiss. Hollow of the knee, thighs. Buss buss. Pearl and mussel.
Amor looks for Psyche. O wondrous catch of fish!
Jubilation and love. The arrow hits the peach. Madame
peels the banana. Buss buss. O wondrous perspiration!
The armpits taste of bitter almond. The peach has no stone.
Madame bites into the banana. The mirror bursts.

HE AND SHE

My little plump cupcake
My rococo popover
My ambrosial creampuff
My fruity air strudel
My fragrant cinnamon bun
My silky blancmange
My sweaty honey cruller
My blond banana split
My velvet spicetart
My swelling peach melba

You nasty nutcracker you
You yellow wineguzzler you
You sad krautpecker you
You uptight breadmunchkin you
You fanatical potatoparson you
You dirty cheddarstomper you
You senile flourgrifter you
You bloody noodlestrainer you
You sticky liverwurstler you
You stupid soup pisser you

translated by Rosmaries Waldrop

Daniel Falb

when signboards blur
the arrival station is hard to pronounce

the regional crop was a resource, the very gesture ethnic
in the accelerating people-go-round and you,
                              which face you ride.
right here began our report on the miss-election.

          before remodeling the hall had temporarily
housed immigrants, and again now.
          we had to leave, you looked simply stunning, or
I did. an international face was certainly

  a gateway to the world, but who could keep watching tv.
and in the open space of these reservations, of the *party*,
we stood kneedeep in the grass and I didn't know
                              where to look.

as far as the doctor series i of course didn't make it.
               shouldn't have repeated myself so much.
but even in farmland
          anamneses are sweeping from village to village
as shooting scripts. that's geographic action.
                    in these lodgings wilhelm conrad röntgen
had invented the sunlamp. stage fright before
     performing. true, the women's jail's a non-stop show,
although, no speaking parts,
                    in the open air, this waiting for the cue.

my personal items seemed out of reach,
                         yet we'd always been cuddly
discarded icons, was that in the politics section or
        in sports. the survey asked *on how many yachts
can you be at the same time,* we checked *yes.*
                         and the endless regatta.
the representative part went may to september,
            afterwards hard to escape our own versions.
where was it i'd put my things. we leafed
        through the *mare* we had found to sleep in.

selecting the maps was not easy. the contour and clearing
of these parks. was this mixed forest.

        foot-paths undermined what's called the coast, and
evenings the whole area blazed with such stupendous,
                     metallic light, its ionic use:
correctly to locate the euro-tunnel.
            far below the threshold of consciousness
action potential remained alien to the space.

                 when signboards blur
the arrival station is hard to pronounce, *mickey*

or so. this meant *not in my backyard,*
            but the buildings were not sketched in,
and sleeping cargo breathes
what no dream has known,
                transmit, transit, transit.

the lading station was set to body temperature, which
didn't mean it was alive.
        money-laundering was here considered molting,
you stood undressed amid the foam.
              we also imported the terrarium dutyfree and
what there shed its skin belonged to both of us.
        money-laundering was here considered molting,
but this sort of thing blows up.
                  we had our hands full with spending.

someone out there was sporting my kidney,
                        and it wasn't you.
your canary looked so peculiar today,
                and your thighs in full bloom,
which in passing i didn't notice.

nights on end the webcam
showed nothing but this lounge, the built-in
materials sympatico
              like the pussy not found here.

goretex, read
up to the first climax after ca. 72 hours,
the really big themes felt good to the touch.

i simply tore down these facings,
i wanted to see the wall,
            that's how i became a stripper.

this here could also
                be a high-end kitchen,
but they are all still up
      in the roof garden, in their new jackets.

the boundaries of your body are identical with the walls of this room,
and the interior makes no difference, the windows
     look like in long car dialogue scenes in older films, the telephone
grafted somehow into this brain as a nerve ending,
          a kind of pain I suppose, a bottle of coke in front of your eyes
and your hand covers the label till you spread your fingers and
              the writing becomes visible, and still in the back of your head
these unending serial images of a gastroscopy, eloquent like a
     western, which is why you hardly leave your dumbbells any more.

you seem hot around the eyes, and it's true, thermal panes
    were installed last summer in the windows, as dressing. but you knew
the test. this random blush. "okay,
after the questioning you looked like a small female victim in the what's-
          what volume *mummies*." giggles. the room temperature remained
constant and low, variations outside noticeable only after
              a delay and in much muted form, which meant rejection.

in the garden, next to the pool, your privatized court of law:
not even the sea gets past security.
    "i…had already heard of these gated communities,…but then
they were not to be found…and my circulation…acted crazy."
your behavior is identified as nonstop publicity. you smile at
the camera and go for a swim, immediately caught in the current.

the bright natural stone used everywhere
        regulates the length of the stay, the adopted child

stands up under upgrade pressure,
    mother, *mall,* where were you, went the announcement.

a cleaning crew pick you up and are
        deported, you shouldn't have gone out there,

it is raining. the whole lot heated,
            quick evaporation and questions

from the retailers' org, now are you or
        are you not my daughter. there were enough

parking spaces still and parks, you wanted a turn at
        the wheel, but could not find the service road.

light weaponry, the zone above your eyes, *commander*
sighted in the sniperscopes, we
too drove toyotas. who was it had taken the brochures
for political formation.
            in german, about the GFR, for example

your somewhat unkempt body,
warm and constitutional, christiane was immediately

shot, i ready to cooperate and very
                very happy.

being this side and that of the diplomatic mission
grounds was but one single long moment.

stop-motion shows figures in strategic position
at the fence, the national territory

       outside as the mission of these grounds, or
how was that again. then shows the cast turn

              liquid, was it the immigrants'
hammer or ... the marshals' sickle.

          could you please remind me
what i thought of this. between

the plantains one can see schlieren of flight gestures,
then i saw red, it was outside i suppose, as was i.

... already single objects entered the frame, buildings
between the glaciers, ambience of the conversation called
instructions for enlarging, "i suddenly feel
     strange, it's coming over me again," pictures of that.
in the analysis of your speech pattern, there emerged first
    a mountainous landscape, high plateaus, then finally
the supply booths of the marathon. "we could
            talk for hours. i always opened up.
so i could get proper treatment," via cellphone
              we could be tracked anywhere.

with raw material in reverse from end product via refinement and
        borders back to timberland etc., the provinces, and the weight
of meals consumed per year, by the truckload, we thought
as children, metabolicly well placed for a smile or good game of tennis.
technique! just technique! *in the beginning* no grounds for aggression, prenatal
simulation of stair-climbing, talks on tape and the monkeys, ah the monkeys.

zero dead, this rule you had followed all along. visible from
    the window a private airfield, logistics apparently arrivals only. un-
simultaneously you lie here in a coma; we, as personnel of this…hotel,
    massage your thighs. arrivals only, that piles up inside the body.
endless occupation of the passageways. once more:
        no-one had died, true, but no-one had got off the ground,
cockpits remained untouched. we let things happen,
            aprons askew, thumbs fucking you.

above ground nothing but assisted living, the outskirts supposed waste land,
you feel up your social worker's skirt
        and pinch her cunt because she's a pet.
this scene at any rate not played before the boss: "they just barged
        in, got nothing left now, am high and dry,
can howl at the moon."
    a kind of light-thread above the juvenile delinquent's head.
a very artistic police photo, this,
        the mark disappeared in retouching.
dogs, rabbits, not out of a hat, but present,
        doorframes custom-made to shoulder height.

fast forward is important for this motion,
        to see: the viscous flow of passers-by
at busy pedestrian crossings.
        co-opted by the highway patrol, videos
for smooth traffic, gray and rather mechanical:
    ptolemy's sun. when buying this middle income car
you install your own extras,
        e.g. electric windows in back, a.c., tempomat.

other rules for proceeding, a change of place.
                    this landscape as unfamiliar as a surgically

altered face. i remember i ought to know you,
                            you're part of the family.

i remember a closeness, OK so you're unknown,
                        but close. (a discontinuity,

an unbelievable acquittal: travel broadens.)
        i was here once before, i must have been here once

before. the left hand goes along the map
                    and finds the road, the right hand

knoweth it not. (anatomy in arms.)
                        a pitiful bullfight in spain.

no exposure, no blur at the forcefeed farms
                                naturalistic scenery.

trickle, economical, beyond the photographic
                            plates. settlements.

a local thunderstorm, bypassing the system sideways.
                                essentially hunting,

fishing, nickel mining. no archeology.
                            environs without

explorers. the space outside the law
            and without precedent. generators

for security, observations in, say, the vegetable garden,
                            the swash biography.

only one region is authorized,
                                    this one.

the subliminal senders we'd put together ourselves. "somewhere
                out there." the cars here in almost military camouflage.
the police radio a revelation. "the voices… always here."
           date and time on record. whoever was fugitive. what was said.
                "hey, the solderin bit's cold, it wonna work, hold on."
images from off. new highways invisible at night.
                forests that, with climate change, shift back and forth.

what settles on your body, which nervous complaint ripples your skin
"as the wind the surface of the sea." go ahead and get proof,
    go see a doctor, you have legs. save the whales, save the underwater
mammals. to hand out flyers, for you. these habits are recessive,
              you say and adjust your bikini, the sea in front of us.
what settles on your *cheek*, somewhere over there the main entrance,
                                      I appreciated that.

                        translated by Rosmarie Waldrop

Raphael Urweider

epitaph
        in memoriam h. c. artmann

thank you i'd rather wear black
wear gray wear colors
of mourning blue and blue
but wishe you everything bright
brighter than hospital white
the tips of first flowers
brighter than snow that
only preserveth love
as felled fish
white as the best of skies
for aeronauts white as paper
now remains having lost color

thank you i'd rather wear black
evening comes in garlands
it is as it should not remain
who says how it should remain
spring's been dismissed
asparagus by asparagus
we ate the spring and wore it thin
i learn what loss
implied what did
loss imply what garlands
promised to evening
asparagus to spring to
wear gray wear colors

of mourning blue and blue
who would not wear mourning's
blue if only for heaven's
sake heavens this sky here a
thin-skinned beast blue
veins of mourning thick blood
of mourning under thin skin
the spectrum of colors in
skies under skin show
the spectrum of mourning
draws to a close the good day
but wishe you everything bright

brighter than hospital white
who wants to sleep away the day
already slept away the night
sun plays away the day
in drapes darkened at
windows silhouettes of brief
visits the sun can't get its way
with drapes at night shadows
stand sleepless in the drapes
in hospitals there is almost no earth
nothing can grow healthy here like
the tips of first flowers

brighter than snow that
just comes to lie here
assumes the color of earth melts
in the sun never rises again
as snow gives up its
lightness as soon as it lies
down grays quickly it falls
on squares on cities on traffic
fades in a breath
if it falls on warm bread
white almost never remaining
only preserveth love

as felled fish
being put on ice
as a whipped dog leaving
town to arrive a proper human
somewhere in the animal kingdom
acknowledged as stateless
and supplied with badges
as cooling metal near my
overheated heart i itch
as a beast as a dog as a fish
white as the best of skies

for aeronauts white as paper
lets get in sir take off in
the beckoning sky light like us
we heat roast lamb
on hotplates in aviaries
brittany's equipped with
good wind we sir with eatables
in professional hands visibility's
good wind sustentive the cliffs
precipitous with calm faces
we see how ash in the air
now remains having lost color

Quanta

PERHAPS IT'S THE COLD THAT MAKES
the windows transparent almost like
water invisible almost and cool

in unobtrusive glasses   the water
we drink that lets pass almost
all light   in waves in particles

hands on panes we suppose some
talk of very tiny events
try to capture them   surmise as glass

can be surmised in windows
as water in a glass   hands almost
always grasp only what's supposed

so we surmise things   talk of events
we want to surmise demonstrate
tiniest things as schemata in the remaining light

in the room   we record   while
solid bodies from outside cast shadows
over the room   remaining water marks the absence

of the glass on the varnish just as the warmth of hands
that long rested there is marked by condensation
a warmth that makes the windows too more visible

WHAT THIS COLOR IS DOING ON THE OUTER WALL
what its condition   how it protects
what its components and if it's

needed   by us in the wider sense
we assess we ask ourselves if the
particles glistening with light emission

on the outer wall are mineral are quartz
or quartzlike silicum maybe and why
we need quartz or silicum maybe

on the outer wall we acknowledge the rough cast
of the wall with our knuckles   and finger
the traces of plaster under the

color on the outer wall whose condition
and function we're not sure of   we test
the glistening particles with our fingers

NO NOT THIS BUTTER LEFT
on the balcony turned
yellow by the light the yellow light

not the bread warm
dried out by the light   though
it smells fresh unlike bread

gone dry indoors   smells because
of the light on afternoon balconies
light that slowly changes color

changes with the speed
of drying and of the color
of goods left out in the light

left out to develop the taste
and smell the particular smell
of dry bread of melted butter

ASTONISHED BY THE MECHANISM   HOW WATER
expands in pressure boilers   grows agitated
in the air and exits as common steam

when pistons cause noise and cries from the
astonished   water suddenly whistles through
horns and signals departure times in fog

present in the air under domes in railroad
stations and harbor-basins precipitates visibly
on windows and other cool surfaces

drips quietly from coats moderately from
half bare trees precisely onto the leaves on the
ground already about to dissolve   water

precipitates in and between them moisture
dampens the noise of any machine   lessens
visibility leaves are crumbled by the hurried steps

of the astonished and the water's own mechanism
inside the leaves   their decay a faint smell of machine
oil of pressure boilers and their smell of steam

water in the air dampens the noise made by
any movement by withdrawing
machines and steps among leaves that decay

SEEING WIND SPEED ON DARK SCREENS
in green letters on ships in headquarters
in the lee   while spindrift sprays stemwards

you step out of the wheelhouse onto the deck into
the wind   small green numbers in front of your eyes
you expect coasts where almost nothing can be expected

and hear the radar's steady echo   and find
in the dark behind the bright spindrift behind the moving
position-lights   what on the screen glows green

translated by Rosmarie Waldrop

NOTES:

The poets in this magazine issue, mostly in their thirties and forties, show great formal diversity. The work ranges from the sound explorations of Anja Utler to the camp sonnets of Ann Cotten; from Czernin's puns and permutations to Rinck's and Falb's deceptively simple *parlando;* from Donhauser's grammatical disruptions to Papenfuss's avant-baroque lists and "sassy East tone." But they all share a concern with form and with language as material. They have also all received at least one prize.

The interested reader might look up these books in English by other poets in this age-group:
Oswald Egger, *Room of Rumor* (trans. Michael Pisaro; Green Integer).
Gerhard Falkner, *Seventeen Selected Poems* (trans. Mark Anderson; quert zui opü).
Dieter Gräf, *Tousled Beauty* (trans. Andrew Shields; Green Integer).
Lutz Seiler, *Poems* (trans. Andrew Duncan; duration press).
—, *In the Year One: Selected Poems* (trans. Tony Frazer, Giramondo, Sydney)
Ulf Stolterfoht, *Lingos I-IX* (trans. Rosmarie Waldrop, Burning Deck).
Peter Waterhouse, *Where Are We Now?* (trans. Rosmarie Waldrop; duration press).

Ongoing sources for German poetry in English:
www.no-mans-land.org/ (German poetry and prose in English translation).
www.lyrikline.org/ (many authors have at least some English versions available on the site).

Ann Cotten was born in 1982 in Iowa, grew up in Vienna from age 5, and now lives in Berlin. Her selection of double sonnets is taken from her first book, *Fremdwörterbuchsonette* (Suhrkamp, 2007). Forthcoming in 2008: *Nach der Welt. Listen in der konkreten Poesie* (Klever Verlag, Wien) and an elegy, *Das Pferd* (SuKuLTuR).

Franz Josef Czernin was born in 1952 in Vienna and now lives mostly in the Steiermark. He has published many books of poetry, essays, aphorisms, like *elemente, sonette* and *das labyrinth erst erfindet den roten faden* (Hanser Verla;g, 2002 and 2005), to mention just two. Our selections are from *gedichte* (Droschl, 1992) and *anna und franz* (Droschl, 1982). Three poems translated by Andrew Duncan are in *Chicago Review: New Writing in German* (Summer 2002).

Michael Donhauser (born 1956) lives in Vienna. He studied German and Romance literatures and has translated poetry by Rimbaud, Francis Ponge and Michael Hamburger. His recent books of poetry include *Schönste Lieder* and *Vom Sehen* (Urs

Engeler, 2007 and 2004). Our texts are taken from *Ich habe lange nicht doch nur an dich gedacht* (Urs Engeler, 2005). Other poems, translated by Andrew Joron, can be found in *Aufgabe* 2 (Spring 2002), and, translated by Ian Galbraith, in *Shearsman* 57 (Winter 2003/04).

Ute Eisinger (born1964) comes from the Lower Austrian wine region and now lives in Vienna. She studied literature and history, writes poems and experimental prose. She has translated Hart Crane's *The Bridge* as well as Dylan Thomas, Ken Babstock and, from the Russian, Ilya Kutik. "projectileArc" is taken from her book *Bogen* (Sisyphus, 2002).

Daniel Falb was born in Kassel in 1977 and lives in Berlin. Has published in journals and anthologies like *Sprache im technischen Zeitalter* and *Jahrbuch der Lyrik* 2006. The sequence "when signboards blur the arrival station is hard to pronounce" is from his first book, *die räumung dieser parks* (kookbooks, 2003).

Hendrik Jackson was born in Düsseldorf in 1971 and lives in Berlin. He is part of the editorial board of the website *www.lyrikkritik.de*. After his first volume of poetry, *einflüsterungen von seitlich* (Morpheo Verlag, 2001), from which our selections are taken, Jackson published *brausende bulgen – 95 Thesen über die Flußwasser in der menschlichen Seele* (2004), *Dunkelströme* (2006) and translations of Marina Tsvetaeva's poetry (2003). Two poems translated by Nicholas Grindell are in *Chicago Review: New Writing in German* (Summer 2002).

Margret Kreidl (1964, Salzburg) lives in Vienna and writes plays, libretti, poems and prose. Our selection is taken from *Laute Paare: Szenen Bilder Listen* (Edition Korrespondenzen, 2002). Other books include: *Ich bin eine Königin* (1996), *In allen Einzelheiten: Katalog* (1998), *Mitten ins Herz* (2005).

Bert Papenfuss (born 1956 in East Germany) began as electrician and sound-&-lighting technician. From 1980 on free-lance writer, often collaborating with rock musicians. He co-edits the cultural-political journal *Gegner* and since 1999 co-manages Kaffee Burger in Berlin. Recent books are *Rumbalotte* (2005), *Astrachan* (2003), and *Haarbogensturz: Versuche über Staat und Welt* (2001). Andrew Duncan's translation is taken from *Rumbalotte Continua* (Verlag Peter Engstler, 2004). Other poems in English can be found in *Sulfur* 27 (Fall 1990) and on websites like http://webdelsol.com/Perihelion/bert.htm

Steffen Popp was born in 1978 in East Germany. He studied German literature and philosophy in Dresden, Leipzig, and Berlin, where he has lived since 2001. In 2004 his collection of poetry *Wie Alpen* appeared, in 2006 the novel *Ohrenberg oder der Weg dorthin* (both kookbooks). "Auratic Agrology" is from his second collection of poems, *Kolonie zur Sonne* (kookbooks, 2008).

Monika Rinck was born in Zweibrücken in 1969. After her university years devoted to history, comparative linguistics and religious studies, she became famous for her *Begriffsstudio*, a collection (and book, 2001) of weird linguistic neologisms discovered in the media. Rosmarie Waldrop's translations are taken from Rinck's first book of poems, *Verzückte Distanzen* (zu Klampen Verlag, 2004); Nicholas Grindell's, from *zum fernbleiben der umarmung* (kookbooks, 2007). Other translations by Grindell were published in *Shearsman* 58 (2004)

Farhad Showghi was born in 1961. After spending his youth in Czechoslovakia, Germany, and finally Iran, he returned in 1978 to Germany to study medicine. He now lives as a poet, translator, and physician in Hamburg. Our text is the title sequence of *Ende des Stadtplans* (Urs Engeler, 2003).

Hans Thill (1954) lives in Heidelberg as a poet, translator (Apollinaire, Félix Fénéon, Queneau, Soupault) and editor/publisher. Tony Frazer's translation, "Change of Location: the Sons," is taken from *Kühle Religionen* (Das Wunderhorn, 2003); Rosmarie Waldrop's selections, from *Zivile Ziele* (Das Wunderhorn, 1995).

Raphael Urweider was born in 1974 in Bern, Switzerland. He sees himself as both poet and musician. He has performed with the Bern Hip-Hop crew LDeeP and composed music for several plays. The sequence "Quanta" is taken from his first volume of poetry, *Lichter in Menlo Park* (Dumont, 2000); "Epitaph," from *Das Gegenteil von Fleisch* (Dumont, 2003). His most recent book is *Alle Deine Namen* (Dumont, 2008).

Anja Utler (1973) lives in Vienna. She studied in Norwich and St. Petersburg and wrote her thesis on Russian women poets of the 20th Century. Both our sequences are taken from *münden — entzüngeln* (Edition Korrespondenzen, 2004). Since then she has published *brinnen* (Korrespondenzen, 2006).

Ron Winkler, born 1973, lives in Berlin where he edits the literary magazine *intendenzen*. Our selections are taken from *vereinzelt Passanten* (kookbooks, 2004) and *Fragmentierte Gewässer* (Berlin Verlag, 2007). Earlier titles are *Morphosen* and *vielleicht ins Denkmal gesetzt* (both 2002). Other poems, translated by Jake D. Schneider, are forthcoming in *Circumference: Poetry in Translation* and *Jubilat*.

Uljana Wolf was born in 1979 in Berlin where she still lives today. Sie studied German and English literature in Berlin and Cracow, and works as a translator and in a bookstore. *kochanie ich habe brot gekauft*, her first book, was published by kookbooks in 2005.
    "erasures," a collaboration with Christian Hawkey, was executed on a bi-lingual edition of Elizabeth Barrett-Browning's *Sonnets from the Portuguese*, translated by Rainer Maria Rilke (*Sonette aus dem Portugiesischen*, Insel Verlag, 1994).

Translators:

Andrew Duncan (born in Leeds, 1956) began with publishing in punk "fanzines" and editing the magazine *Angel Exhaust*. His books of poetry include *In a German Hotel* (Ochre, 1978), *Cut Memories and False Commands* (Reality Studios, 1991), *Sound Surface* (Five Eyes of Wiwaxia, 1992), *Alien Skies* (Equipage, 1992), *Pauper Estate*, and *Switching and Main Exchange* (both Shearsman, 2000). His Selected Poems, *Anxiety Before Entering a Room*, is out from Salt Publishing (2001), as is his literary/ cultural criticism, *The Failure of Conservatism in Modern British Poetry* (2003). Learns European languages as a hobby and has worked on translations of Thomas Kling, Lutz Seiler, and Ulf Stolterfoht, in particular.

Tony Frazer, born in the UK in 1951, is editor/publisher of *Shearsman* magazine and Shearsman Books. He edited the anthology *A State of Independence* (Stride, 1998), Roy Fisher's *Interviews Through Time, & Selected Prose* (Shearsman, 2000), and co-edited *Chicago Review's New Writing in German* (2002). He translates from German and Spanish. His translation of Lutz Seiler's *In the Year One: Selected Poems* was published by Giramondo in Sydney in 2005. Most recently he has edited and translated a series of classic texts for Shearsman Books, including *Spanish Poetry of the Golden Age* (2008).

Nicholas Grindell (UK) has been working in Berlin as a translator since 1993. His poetry translations have appeared in *Chicago Review, Shearsman*, and *No Man's Land*. He has translated plays for the London stage, worked on the English edition of the *Frankfurter Allgemeine Zeitung* (published with the *International Herald Tribune*), and edited the three-issue magazine *Abweichende Linienführung* (epram.org).

Christian Hawkey is the author of *The Book of Funnels* (Verse Press, 2004), the chapbook *HourHour*, (Delirium Press, 2005), and *Citizen Of* (Wave Books, 2007). He is currently a DAAD Artist-in-Berlin Fellow.

Rosmarie Waldrop's recent books of poetry are *Curves to the Apple, Blindsight* (New Directions), and *Love, Like Pronouns* (Omnidawn). U of Alabama Press published *Dissonance (if you are interested): Collected Essays* (2005). Recent translations: Ulf Stolterfoht's *Lingos I-IX*, Gerhard Rühm's *i my feet* (both Burning Deck) and, with Keith Waldrop, Jacques Roubaud's *The Form of a City Changes Faster, Alas, Than the Human Heart* (Dalkey Archive).

SERIE d'ECRITURE
[Nos. 1-5: Spectacular Diseases, Peterborough, UK; No. 6- : Burning Deck}

No. 1: Alain Veinstein, *Archeology of the Mother* (trans. Tod Kabza, R. Waldrop), 1986

No. 2: Emmanuel Hocquard, *Late Additions* (trans. Connell McGrath, R. Waldrop), 1988

No. 3: Anne-Marie Albiach, Marcel Cohen, Jean Daive, Dominique Fourcade, Jean Frémon, Paol Keineg, Jacqueline Risset, Jacques Roubaud, Claude Royet-Journoud (trans. Anthony Barnett, Charles Bernstein, Lydia Davis, Serge Gavronsky, Rachel Stella, Keith & Rosmarie Waldrop), 1989

No. 4: Anne-Marie Albiach, Olivier Cadiot, Danielle Collobert, Edith Dahan, Serge Fauchereau, Dominique Fourcade, Liliane Giraudon, Joseph Guglielmi, Vera Linhartova, Anne Portugal (trans. Charles Bernstein, Norma Cole, Robert Kocik, Natasha, Ron Padgett, Keith & Rosmarie Waldrop), 1990

No. 5: Joseph Guglielmi, *Dawn* (trans. Rosmarie Waldrop), 1991

No. 6: Jean Daive, *A Lesson in Music* (trans. Julie Kalendek), 1992

No. 7: Pierre Alferi, Jean-Pierre Boyer, Olivier Cadiot, Dominique Fourcade, Jean Frémon, Jean-Marie Gleize, Dominique Grandmont, Emmanuel Hocquard, Isabelle Howald, Anne Portugal, Jacques Roubaud, James Sacré, Anne Talvaz, Esther Tellerman (trans. David Ball, Norma Cole, Stacy Doris, Paul Green, Tom Mandel, Pam Rehm, Cole Swensen, Keith & Rosmarie Waldrop), 1993

No. 8: Paol Keineg, *Boudica* (trans. Keith Waldrop), 1994

No. 9: Marcel Cohen, *The Peacock Emperor Moth* (trans. Cid Corman), 1995

No. 10: Jacqueline Risset, *The Translation Begins* (trans. Jennifer Moxley), 1996

No. 11: Alain Veinstein, *Even a Child* (trans. Robert Kocik, Rosmarie Waldrop), 1997

No. 12: Emmanuel Hocquard, *A Test of Solitude* (trans. Rosmarie Waldrop), 2000

No. 13/14: *Crosscut Universe: Writing on Writing from France* (ed./trans. Norma Cole), 2000: Anne-Marie Albiach, Joë Bousquet, Danielle Collobert, Edith Dahan, Jean Daive, André du Bouchet, Dominique Fourcade, Liliane Giraudon, Joseph Guglielmi, Emmanuel Hocquard, Roger Laporte, Roger Lewinter, Raquel, Mitsou Ronat, Jacques Roubaud, Agnès Rouzier, Claude Royet-Journoud

No. 15: Pascal Quignard, *On Wooden Tablets: Apronenia Avitia* (trans. Bruce X), 2001

No. 16: Esther Tellermann, *Mental Ground* (trans. Keith Waldrop), 2002

No. 17: Pierre Alferi, *OXO* (trans. Cole Swensen), 2004

No. 18: Jean Grosjean, *An Earth of Time* (trans. Keith Waldrop), 2006

No. 19: Suzanne Doppelt, *Ring Rang Wrong* (trans. Cole Swensen), 2006

No. 20: Caroline Dubois, *You Are the Business* (trans. Cole Swensen), 2008

No. 21: Isabelle Baladine Howald, *Secret of Breath* (trans. Eléna Rivera), 2008

  Chapbook Supplements:

No. 1: Claude Royet-Journoud, *i.e.* (trans. Keith Waldrop), 1995

No. 2: Pascal Quignard, *Sarx* (trans. Keith Waldrop), 1997

No. 3: Anne-Marie Albiach, *A Geometry* (trans. Keith & Rosmarie Waldrop), 1998

No. 4: Marie Borel, *Close Quote* (trans. Keith Waldrop), 2003